✳ THE BEST OF ✳
STUNTOLOGY

✳ THE BEST OF ✳
STUNT
OLOGY

304 PRANKS, TRICKS & CHALLENGES
TO AMUSE & ANNOY YOUR FRIENDS

Sam Bartlett

WORKMAN PUBLISHING ✳ NEW YORK

Dedicated to Julie Belcher.

Library of Congress Cataloging-in-Publication Data is available.
ISBN-13: 978-0-7611-4978-1

Cover art by Sam Bartlett

Author photo by Abby Ladin
Additional credits on page 316

Workman books are available at special discounts when purchased in bulk for
premiums and sales promotions as well as for fund-raising or educational use.
Special editions or book excerpts can also be created to specification.
For details, contact the Special Sales Director at the address below.

Workman Publishing Company
225 Varick Street
New York, NY 10014-4381
www. workman.com

Printed in the United States of America
First printing February 2008

10 9 8 7 6 5 4 3 2 1

CONTENTS

AN INTRODUCTION TO STUNTOLOGY

SHELBURNE, VERMONT, 1967. I WAS SIX YEARS OLD WHEN MY MOTHER SHOWED ME HOW TO PIN A GLASS OF WATER TO THE CEILING.

IT DOESN'T!

I CAN'T BELIEVE THAT ACTUALLY WORKS!

SPLASH!

A STUNTOLOGIST IS BORN.

THE SAFETY PINS ACTUALLY HOLD THE FULL GLASS OF WATER TO THE CEILING. I'LL SHOW YOU.

WOW...

MY PARENTS HOSTED PARTIES FOR FACULTY AND GRADUATE STUDENTS IN MY FATHER'S DEPARTMENT AT THE UNIVERSITY, AND THEY LOVED PRACTICAL JOKES.

TRY IT ONE MORE TIME, SERGEI. YOU'LL GET THE QUARTER INTO THE FUNNEL THIS TIME (ALONG WITH THE REST OF MY DRINK!).

MY FAMILY VALUED THE PURSUIT OF OBSCURE KNOWLEDGE AND ABILITIES.

I'M GOING TO BED!

HOW LONG IS THIS GOING TO TAKE?

MY FATHER BOILING WATER IN A PLASTIC BAG OVER A CANDLE FLAME.

GET YOUR FEET OFF THE TABLE!

plinkety plink plink

AS A TEENAGER I TAUGHT MYSELF TO PLAY THE BANJO.

I GOT MYSELF THROUGH COLLEGE BY PLAYING THE BANJO, DRAWING, AND GETTING INVOLVED WITH (G)BAMAS, BURLINGTON AMATEUR MUTUAL AMUSEMENT SOCIETY. *

SHE STEPPED OUT OF THE ONION RING. DISQUALIFIED!

LET'S PLAY CHEEK DARTS NEXT!

* THE "G" IS SILENT.

I PUT MY DEGREE IN GEOGRAPHY TO GOOD USE AND BECAME A FULL-TIME TOURING MUSICIAN.

WE JUST CROSSED THE STATE LINE!

WHOO-HOO! WE'RE IN OKLAHOMA!

WHERE IN OKLAHOMA?

SOMEWHERE IN OKLAHOMA, I DON'T KNOW...

DON'T YOU KNOW HE CAN'T REALLY READ MAPS?

I THOUGHT HE WAS A GEOGRAPHY MAJOR OR SOMETHING.

HEY... LAY OFF!

1 MILDLY ANNOYING TO HIGHLY IRRITATING

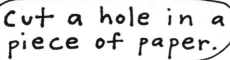

Cut a hole in a piece of paper.

say to a friend, "I can poke your entire head through this tiny hole in the paper."

"No, you can't"

They will say incorrectly.

Then begin methodically poking every square inch of the person's head through the hole in the paper with your finger.

poke poke

LAST CLAP FIRST CLAP STUNT

IF YOU'RE AT A FORMAL CONCERT AND BORED OUT OF YOUR SKULL,

YOU CAN PLAY THE GAME OF FIRST CLAP/ LAST CLAP.

WHEN A PIECE IS OVER, YOU TRY TO BE THE FIRST TO CLAP.

Clap

AND WHEN THE APPLAUSE IS DYING DOWN, YOU TRY TO BE THE LAST PERSON TO CLAP.

Clap!

THE GAME IS MOST FUN IF NO ONE KNOWS YOU'RE PLAYING IT.

KNUCKLE-POCKET POPPING

PUT YOUR LEFT HAND IN FRONT OF YOU LIKE THIS: (MAKE A FIST.)

PLACE YOUR RIGHT HAND ON TOP OF YOUR LEFT. (WITH RIGHT HAND'S MIDDLE FINGER RESTING IN BETWEEN MIDDLE AND RING FINGER OF THE LEFT.)

SLIDE THE RIGHT INDEX FINGER OVER THE TOP OF THE RIGHT MIDDLE FINGER USING A LOT OF FRICTION,

AND HAVE IT LAND IN THE LITTLE POCKET BETWEEN THE LEFT HAND'S MIDDLE AND INDEX FINGER KNUCKLES.

POCK!

DONE CORRECTLY, THIS ACTION WILL YIELD A SATISFYING AND ANNOYING "POCK" SOUND.

POCK POCK POCK POCK!

IT'S 3 A.M. PLEASE STOP POCKING.

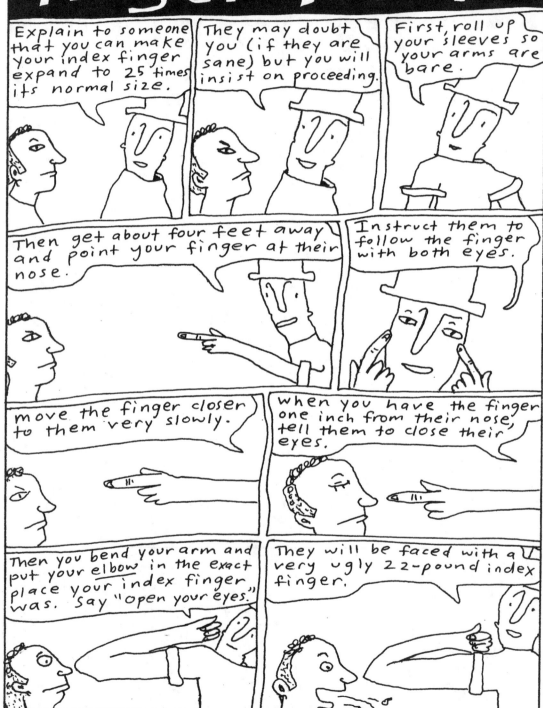

AssisTED-WALKING STUNT

You are walking with a friend. Let them get a little ahead of you.

when they have one foot forward and the back foot is just lifting up to step forward,

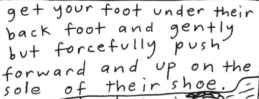
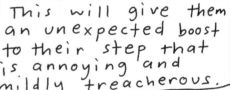

get your foot under their back foot and gently but forcefully push forward and up on the sole of their shoe.

This will give them an unexpected boost to their step that is annoying and mildly treacherous.

MILDLY ANNOYING TO HIGHLY IRRITATING

13

NOSE-BLOWING STUNT

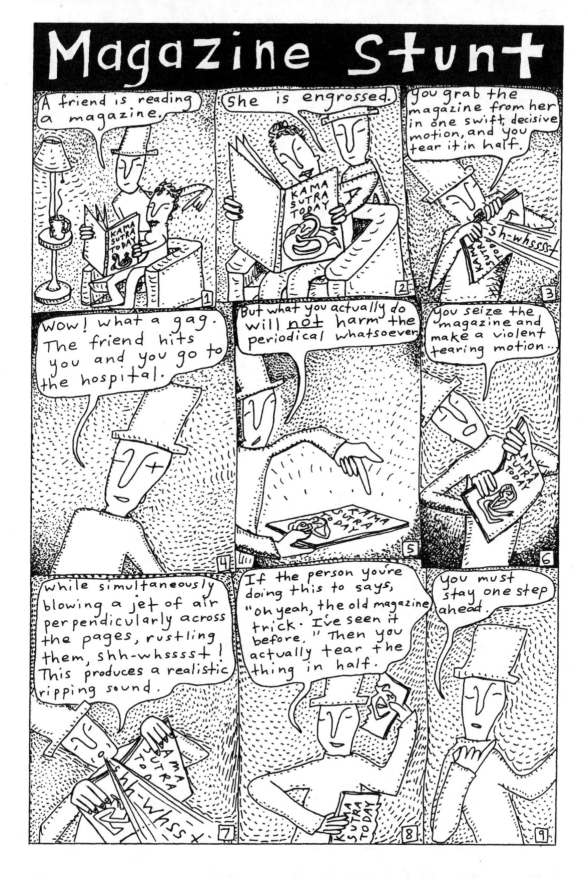

ONE-ARMED CHANGE COUNTER

UNZIP YOUR FLY.

TAKE ONE ARM OUT OF ITS SLEEVE AND HIDE IT INSIDE YOUR SHIRT.

WALK INTO A STORE AND BUY SOME COFFEE. HAND THE SHOPKEEPER SOME MONEY, BUT NOT QUITE ENOUGH TO COVER THE COST.

WHEN YOU ARE ASKED FOR THE REST OF THE MONEY, PULL SOME CHANGE OUT OF YOUR POCKET WITH YOUR GOOD ARM.

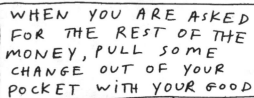

LOOK AT YOUR GOOD ARM AND THEN GLANCE HELPLESSLY AT YOUR EMPTY SHIRT SLEEVE.

THEN: POKE YOUR INDEX FINGER OUT YOUR FLY AND SIFT MATTER-OF-FACTLY THROUGH THE CHANGE.

VERY FUNNY MISTER.

BATHROOM STUNT

Over the course of several weeks or months enter the bathroom while a friend is in the shower.

Develop a pattern of your normal presence in the bathroom while this person showers, so you being there is not a cause for suspicion.

♪

Then one day fill a big cup with ice-cold water while this person is showering,

and nonchalantly pour the cup of cold water over the curtain and onto your unfortunate victim's hind and front quarters.

Aiiiiiiiiiiii!!

PEANUT-BLOWING STUNT

CONCEAL A DOUBLE HANDFUL OF STYRO-FOAM PACKAGING PEANUTS.

GO UP TO SOME-ONE (JUDGE, SENATOR, PRO-FESSIONAL WRESTLER)

PRETEND TO SNEEZE AND BLOW PEANUTS ALL OVER THE PERSON.

RUN.

TONGUE-THROUGH-THE-NAPKIN STUNT

DRAW A LARGE FACE ON A NAPKIN. SPREAD THE NAPKIN ACROSS YOUR OWN FACE.

LEAN YOUR TONGUE AGAINST THE MOUTH HOLE ON THE DRAWING.

YOUR TONGUE WILL EVENTUALLY SOAK THROUGH THE FLIMSY PAPER AND PROTRUDE FROM THE NAPKIN FACE.

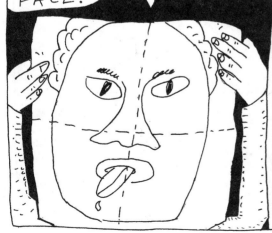

MOVE IT AROUND. FAKE DRAWING, REAL TONGUE. DISGUSTING!

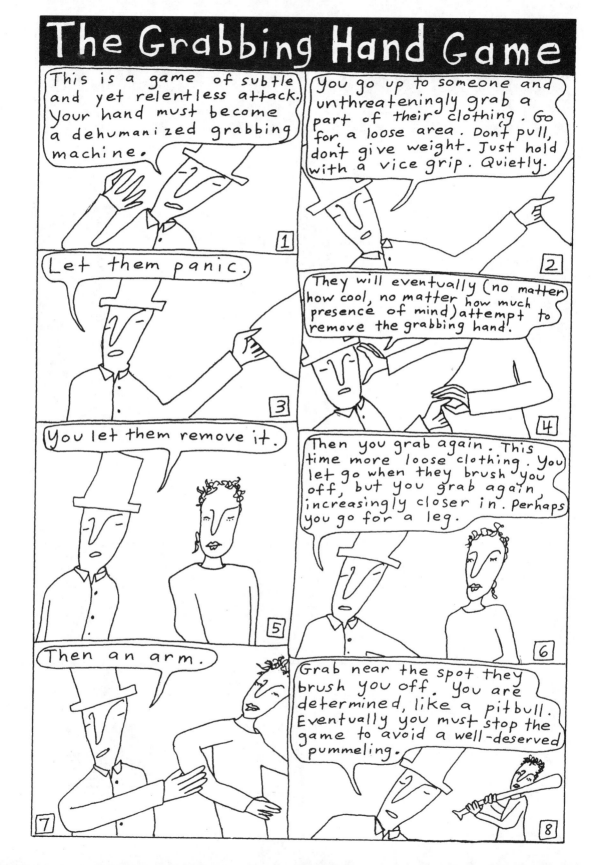

PENCIL-BREAKING STUNT

IN SIXTH GRADE, IF SOMEONE HAD A NEW PENCIL, WE WOULD COME UP TO THEM AND SAY, "HEY, CAN I BORROW THAT?"

AND THEN WE WOULD HOLD THE PENCIL BETWEEN OUR FINGERS IN ONE OF TWO POSITIONS..

1.

2.

THEN SMASH THE HAND HOLDING THE PENCIL DOWN ONTO THE DESKTOP. THE PENCIL WOULD BREAK INTO TWO OR MORE PIECES.

Hey! Dude what are you doing?

Ka-pow!

WE CONTINUED THIS PROTEST AGAINST NEW PENCILS FOR MOST OF THE YEAR UNTIL ONE GUY WHO'D BEEN VICTIMIZED ONE TOO MANY TIMES BEGAN BRINGING IN THESE ENORMOUS PENCILS, THE KIND YOU'RE ISSUED IN FIRST GRADE.

uh-oh

WE TRIED UNSUCCESSFULLY TO BREAK THESE PENCILS, AND THE RITUAL QUIETLY DIED OUT.

LEG HUG
you're about to hug someone, closing in for the embrace.
you
your victim
In the last second, you put your leg up on their shoulder! This is not nearly as hard as you would think.
you do have to be a bit limber to execute this thing, and you must make sure the person you're doing it to is not a member of the Chicago Bulls.

IRRITATING HAND-CLAPPING STUNT

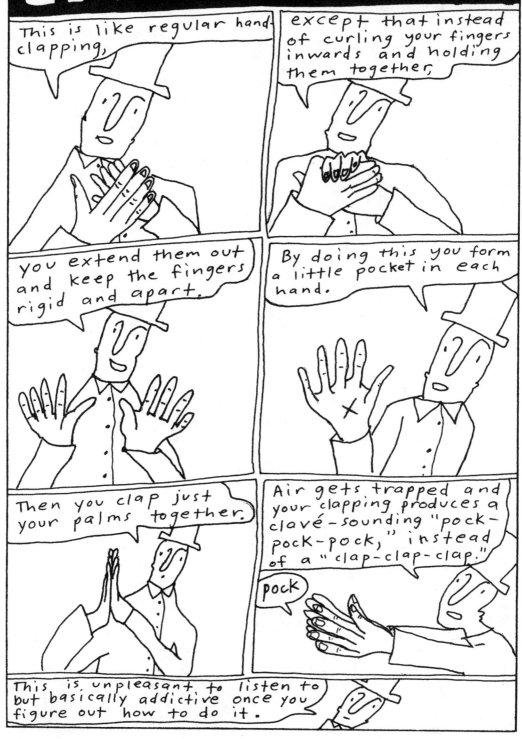

This is like regular hand-clapping,

except that instead of curling your fingers inwards and holding them together,

you extend them out and keep the fingers rigid and apart.

By doing this you form a little pocket in each hand.

Then you clap just your palms together.

Air gets trapped and your clapping produces a clavé-sounding "pock-pock-pock," instead of a "clap-clap-clap."

pock

This is unpleasant to listen to but basically addictive once you figure out how to do it.

Milk Cartons, Exploding

Get a half-pint carton of milk.

Drink the milk.

Close the pouring end.

Flatten out the top.

Turn it upside down.

Slam your fist down on the carton.

PFFT POW

This should produce a satisfying explosion and only a minor spraying of milk.

SPIT OUT GIANT TEETH

WHILE WALKING WITH A GROUP OF PEOPLE DOWN THE STREET,

SECRETLY FILL YOUR MOUTH WITH ALTOID MINTS.

THEN PRETEND TO WALK INTO A STOP SIGN. (KICK THE BASE OF THE SIGN AS YOU DO THIS, TO MAKE IT GO "CLANG!")

FALL BACK, CLUTCHING YOUR MOUTH.

SPIT OUT THE ALTOIDS SLOWLY,

SAYING:

MY TEETH! MY PRECIOUS TEETH!

THIS IS MOST FUNNY BECAUSE ALTOIDS DO NOT REALLY LOOK MUCH LIKE TEETH.

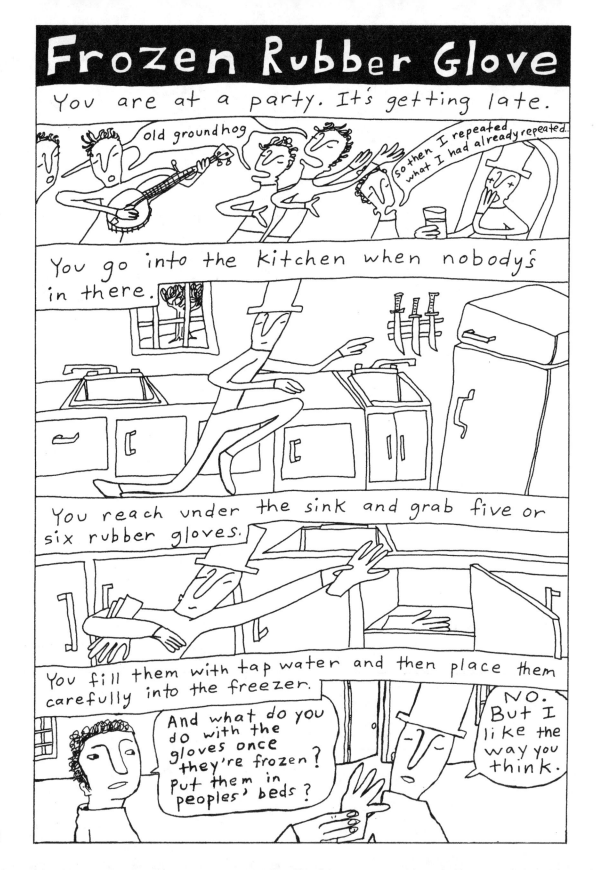

Dandelion Magnetism

This is a perfect springtime stunt. Play it on a friend with a good sense of humor, or someone who already regards himself as a victim.

You need: a dandelion flower, a dandelion seed head, and a fool.

The dialogue might go something like this:

Did you know that you can hide a dandelion flower <u>anywhere</u> on your body and the seed head can always find it?

This seems impossible to me but I'm willing to go along with it for the purposes of this cartoon.

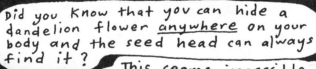

Go ahead. Try it. I won't look. (and you don't have to)

He hides it in his shoe.

Now, with the seed head, carefully move around the surface of his body, pausing here and there. [try to avoid any place the flower might actually be] vibrate the seed head a little from time to time. Finally you come to the mouth...

It's not in your mouth is it?

They open their mouth wide to show how empty it is, and then in goes the seed head, wiggle-wiggle: dandelion fluff all over their bicuspids and uvula. Ha ha ha.

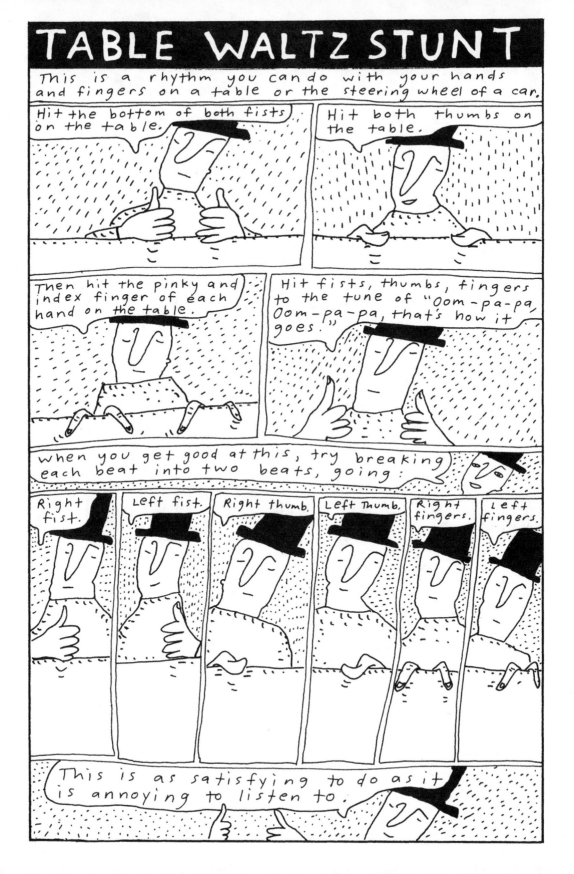

OPEN-A-BOTTLE-WITH-YOUR-EYE-SOCKET-STUNT

SECRETLY TAKE THE CAP OFF A BOTTLE AND THEN GENTLY SCREW IT BACK ON.

GO UP TO SOME FRIENDS, OFFER THEM A DRINK. GIVE THEM THEIR BOTTLE AS WELL AS A BOTTLE OPENER.

THEN NONCHALANTLY HOLD THE BOTTLE UP TO YOUR EYE AND BEAR DOWN ON THE CAP WITH YOUR EYE SOCKET.

TWIST THE BOTTLE WHILE SIMULTANEOUSLY MAKING A "PSHHH" SOUND.

PSHHH

THROW THE CAP OVER YOUR SHOULDER WITH A TOSS OF THE HEAD.

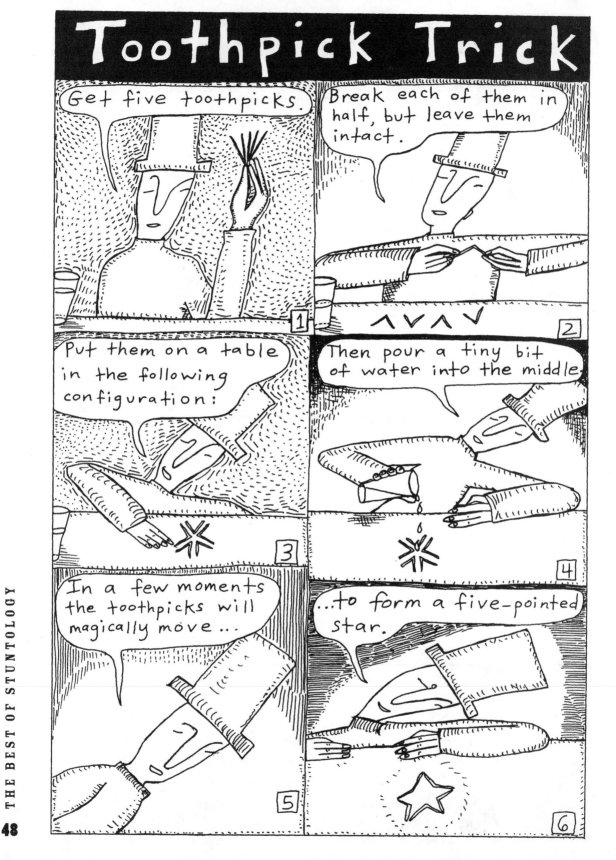

NOSE HAIR PLUCKING

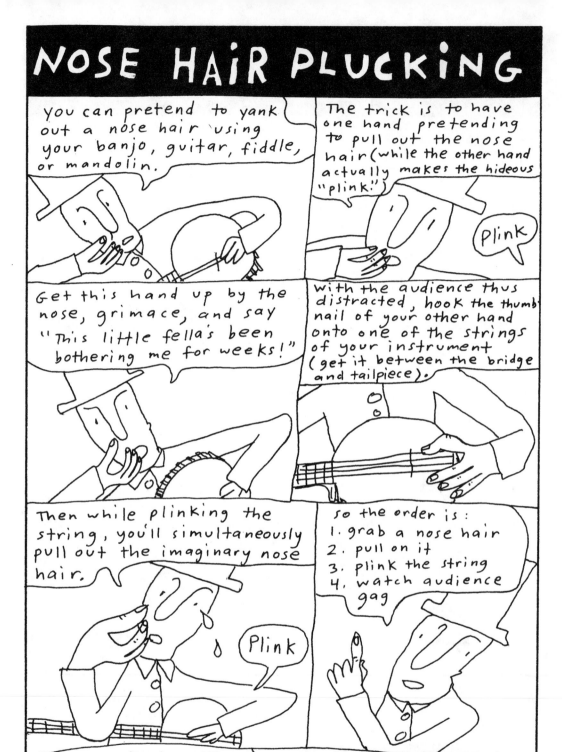

You can pretend to yank out a nose hair using your banjo, guitar, fiddle, or mandolin.

The trick is to have one hand pretending to pull out the nose hair (while the other hand actually makes the hideous "plink.")

Plink

Get this hand up by the nose, grimace, and say "This little fella's been bothering me for weeks!"

With the audience thus distracted, hook the thumbnail of your other hand onto one of the strings of your instrument (get it between the bridge and tailpiece).

Then while plinking the string, you'll simultaneously pull out the imaginary nose hair.

Plink

So the order is:
1. grab a nose hair
2. pull on it
3. plink the string
4. watch audience gag

This stunt also works well to simulate the plucking out of an armpit or pubic hair.

plinkk!

PAPER CLIP STUNT

GET A DOLLAR BILL AND TWO PAPER CLIPS.

FOLD THE DOLLAR ONCE AND ATTACH THE PAPER CLIP AT POINT A.

FOLD IT AGAIN AND ATTACH THE OTHER PAPER CLIP AT POINT B.

GRAB THE ENDS OF THE DOLLAR BILL AND PULL.

THE SEPARATE PAPER CLIPS WILL SLIDE TOGETHER AND MYSTERIOUSLY ATTACH TO ONE ANOTHER.

WHY DOES THIS WORK?

YOU KNOW, WHEN IT COMES RIGHT DOWN TO IT, NO ONE REALLY UNDERSTANDS HOW PAPER CLIPS WORK.

FAMOUS PAPER CLIP-OLOGIST. ↓

AND THAT, MY FRIEND, IS COMPLETE AND UTTER RUBBISH.

FORK TELEKINESIS

YOU WILL NEED TWO FORKS AND A CLOTH NAPKIN.

WEDGE THE HANDLE OF ONE OF THE FORKS BETWEEN THE TINES OF THE OTHER FORK.

HOLD THIS FORKED FORK COMBO IN YOUR RIGHT HAND WHILE SUSPENDING THE CLOTH NAPKIN BETWEEN YOUR HANDS.

SLOWLY SWIVEL THE FORK COMBO UNTIL ONE OF THE FORKS PEEPS ABOVE THE NAPKIN.

IT WILL NOT BE OBVIOUS TO YOUR AUDIENCE HOW THE FORK IS HOVERING ABOVE THE NAPKIN.

PUSH THE FORK UP.

LET IT DOWN.

CONCENTRATE!

SCRATCH SCRATCH

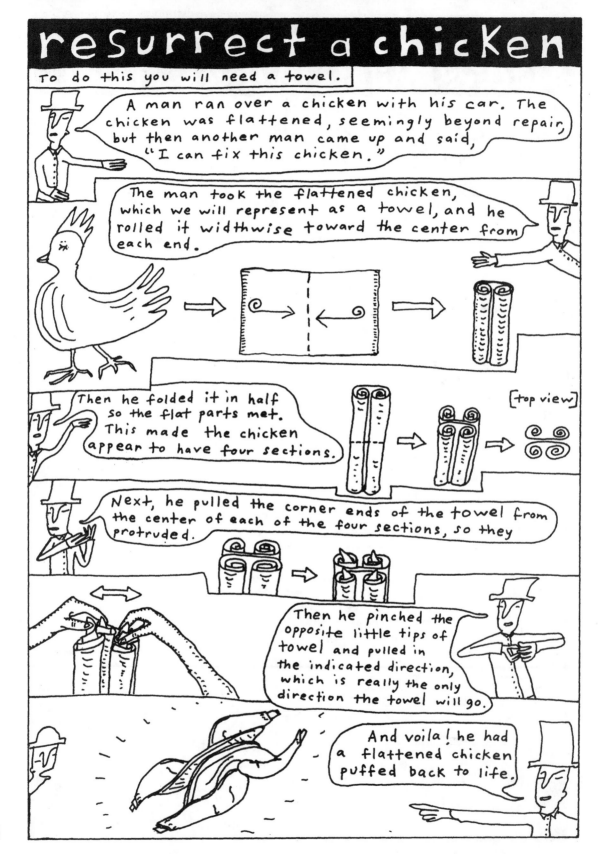

Resurrect a Toothpick

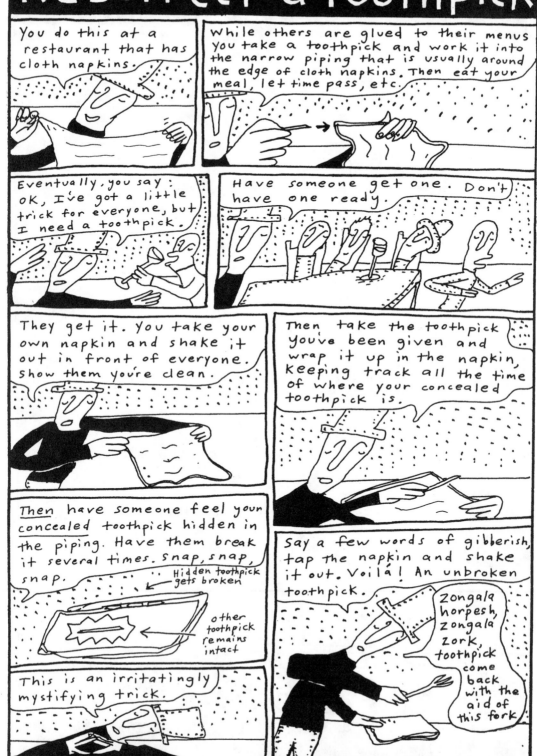

FACE-REVERSAL STUNT

FIND A DISCARDED GLAMOUR MAGAZINE WITH BIG GLOSSY PHOTOS.

SELECT A PHOTO AND CUT OUT THE EYES AND MOUTH.

FLIP THE EYES AND MOUTH UPSIDE-DOWN AND TAPE THEM BACK IN PLACE.

KEEP THE ALTERED PHOTO UPSIDE DOWN AND SHOW IT TO SOMEONE. IT WILL LOOK NORMAL.

THEN PUT IT RIGHT SIDE UP AND THE REVERSED EYES AND MOUTH...

WILL MAKE THE GLAMOUROUS MODEL LOOK LIKE A DEADLY BEAST.

SKEWER THROUGH A BALLOON

GET A SHARP WOODEN BARBEQUE SKEWER AND AN INFLATED BALLOON. GET SOME DISH SOAP WHILE YOU'RE AT IT.

BLAH

PUT A TINY BIT OF DISH SOAP ONTO YOUR FINGERS AND RUB IT ALL OVER THE SKEWER.

HOLD THE BALLOON WITH YOUR LEFT ARM (AWAY FROM YOUR FACE) AND HOLD THE SKEWER WITH THE FINGERS OF THE RIGHT HAND.

TWIST THE SHARP END OF THE SKEWER INTO THE BALLOON. THIS CREATES A CERTAIN AMOUNT OF TENSION IN ANY AUDIENCE.

DONE GENTLY AND STEADILY YOU'LL BE ABLE TO WORK THE SKEWER IN ONE END OF THE BALLOON AND OUT THE OTHER SIDE AND STILL KEEP THE BALLOON INFLATED.

THIS STUNT IS GREAT WHEN IT WORKS, BUT EVEN FUNNIER WHEN IT DOESN'T WORK.

BLAM!

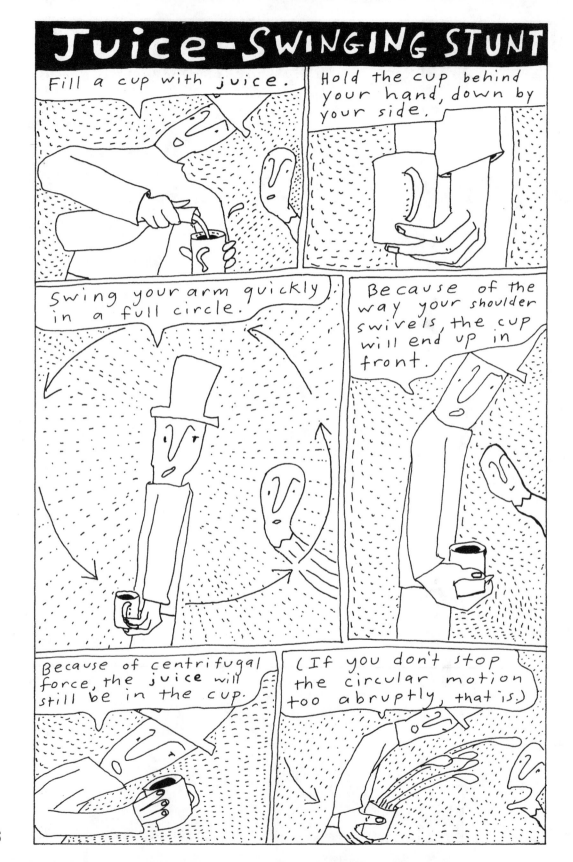

Pick up a bottle

Get a straw and a bottle of something (beer, root beer, birch beer, etc.)

challenge someone to pick up the bottle using only a straw.

Then demonstrate: Bend and insert straw.

Lift. Note the knitting of eyebrows and looks of intense disbelief on the faces of the onlookers.

TA DA!

ZZZ

GRINNING JACKSON STUNT

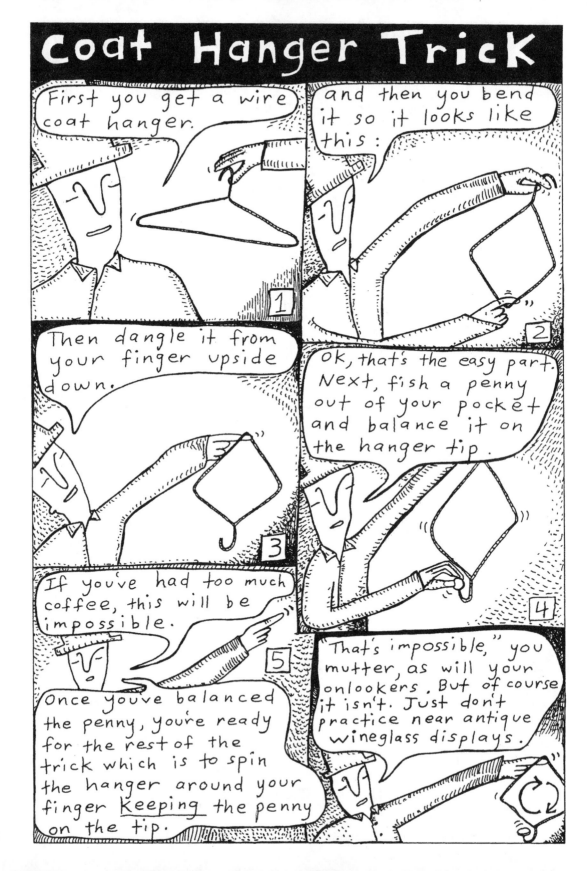

Slow can crush

Stand an empty can on the floor.

Supporting yourself with a couple of chairs, stand on the can. Put very little weight on it.

Then gradually distribute your weight over to the can.

If you do this just right, you will be able to crush the can into itself, and you'll be left with a very solidly accordioned aluminum disk.

TABLE-LIFTING STUNT

You can lift a small table with a pint glass.

Put a sopping wet napkin on a table. Light a match and stand it up on the napkin so it keeps burning.

Place a pint glass over the match. Push down hard with the glass to make a good seal.

Wait for the match to burn out on its own. You will create an impressive vacuum if you do this correctly.

Then lift the glass straight up. (Don't tilt it or you'll break the seal) You should be able to pick up the table with the glass.

Lift carefully. If the seal breaks and you're smiling as you do the stunt -- which you should be doing -- you could knock out an entire row of teeth.

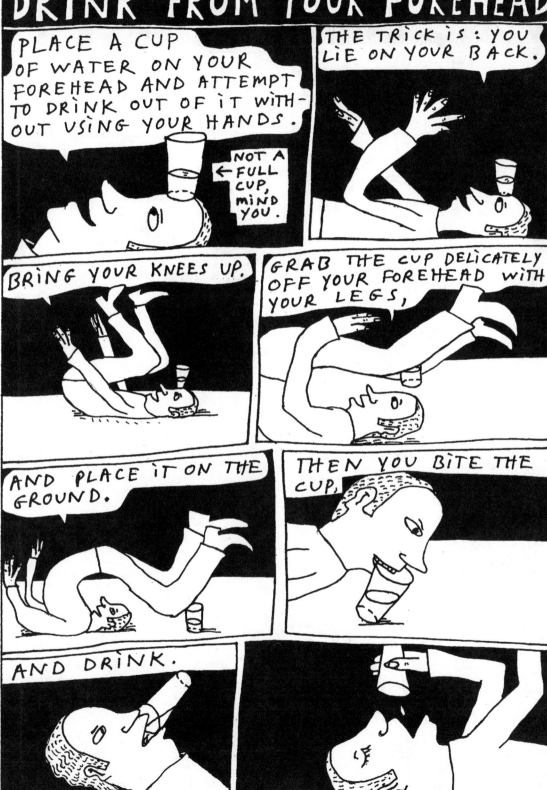

BOTTLE STUNT

Set up two bottles mouth to mouth with a dollar bill between them.

Challenge someone to remove the dollar without knocking over the bottles.

The trick is to grip the dollar firmly at point A, with one hand, and then to strike the bill sharply at point B with the index finger of the other hand.

make sure the bottles are dry against the dollar--no moisture whatsoever-- or you will succeed only in flipping one of the bottles across the room.

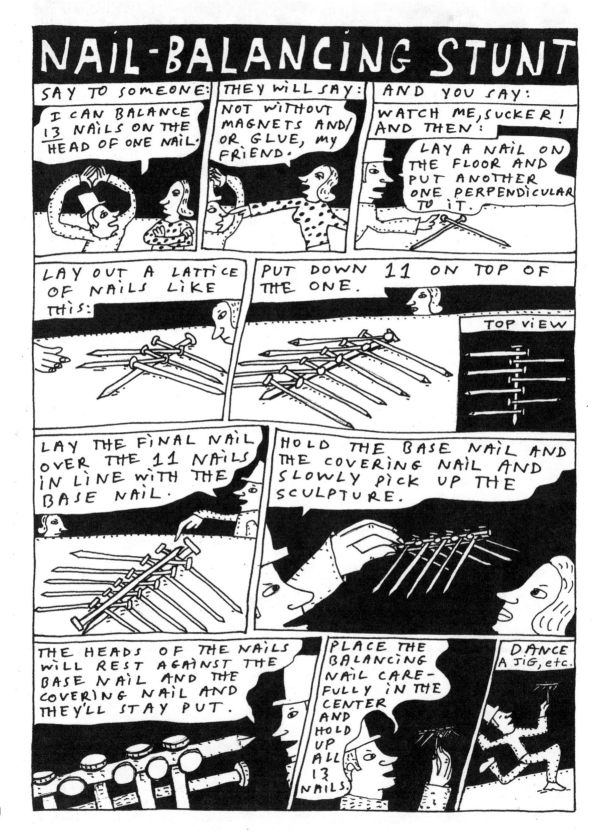

BACK-TO-THE-WALL STUNT

HAVE SOMEONE STAND WITH THEIR BACK TO A WALL.

PLACE A DOLLAR BILL AT THEIR FEET.

SAY: YOU CAN HAVE THE DOLLAR IF YOU CAN TOUCH IT WITH YOUR HANDS, BUT YOUR HEELS, BACK, AND HEAD MUST STAY IN CONTACT WITH THE WALL AT ALL TIMES.

ka-ching!

JUST TO KEEP THINGS INTERESTING, ADD THAT IF BY ANY CHANCE THEY CAN'T REACH IT, THEY MUST GIVE YOU THEIR HOUSE AND LAND.

Impossible Cork Stunt

This is a party trick. You'll need an empty bottle of wine and its cork.

challenge someone to shove the cork back into the bottle. All the way in. They might think this is the stunt.

After they've done it, you tell them, "I can remove the cork using only this cloth napkin." (Hopefully it's a nice party and there are cloth napkins all over the place.)

You prepare the napkin by folding two of the ends towards the middle.

Et voilà!

Put one tip of the folded napkin into the wine bottle. Get the cork to rest in the middle of the cloth, a few inches from the end.

When the cork is positioned, pull slowly and firmly. The cork will come out with the napkin.

Sol's Paper Trick

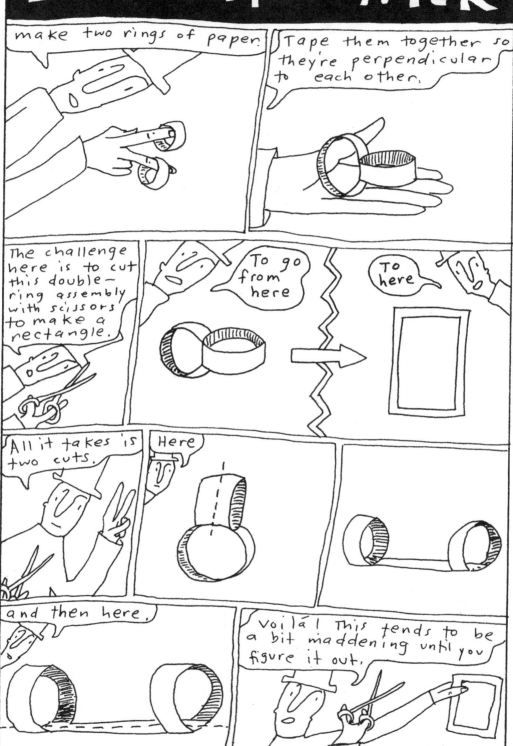

Can-Balancing Stunt

PRANKS, GAGS & TRICKS 3

Medicine Cabinet Stunt

You're having a big party.

Take down the medicine cabinet you have on your bathroom wall.

Remove all the medicine.

Fill the entire cabinet with marbles.

Latch it shut. Put it back on the wall.

Everyone at your party will hear the explosion of marbles when the nosy bastard is caught trespassing in your private pharmacological turf.

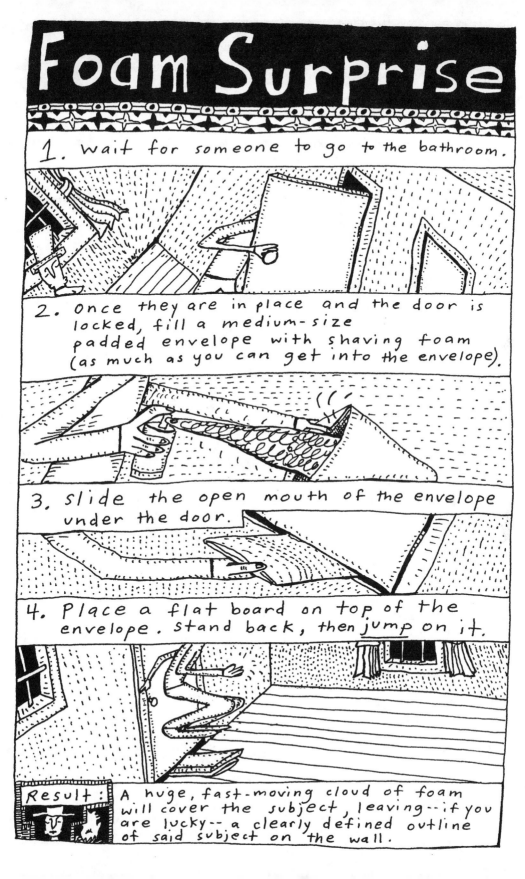

Foam Surprise

1. Wait for someone to go to the bathroom.

2. Once they are in place and the door is locked, fill a medium-size padded envelope with shaving foam (as much as you can get into the envelope).

3. Slide the open mouth of the envelope under the door.

4. Place a flat board on top of the envelope. Stand back, then jump on it.

Result: A huge, fast-moving cloud of foam will cover the subject, leaving--if you are lucky-- a clearly defined outline of said subject on the wall.

Spray Head Surprise

As basic as this trick is, it's worth its weight in shekels.

You'll need a kitchen sink that has one of those spray heads.

And you'll need a rubber band.

Need I say more?

you fasten down the lever on the spray handle so it's stuck on spray, and aim it toward the person who's using the sink.

When they turn on the water to fill the teapot, they'll have a stream of water attacking them.

Good God!

Pre-Sliced Banana

I unpeeled a banana once and watched it fall to the floor in four distinct cylindrical pieces. I was a victim of the mysterious pre-sliced banana stunt.

1

To do this maneuver you need only a banana and a large pin.

2

You insert the pin at various points along the banana and at each spot, wiggle it back and forth in one plane.

3

This process separates the banana into sections while leaving the peel essentially intact.

4

It is important to have a victim for your banana soon after you make your incisions, because the banana will fuse back together before long.

No, not that banana. Try THIS one.

5

The beauty of this stunt is that when someone opens a banana and it tumbles in pieces to the floor, they do not suspect foul play. Why would anyone tamper with a banana? <u>How</u> would anyone tamper with a banana? So they stare at the banana and just don't know what to make of it.

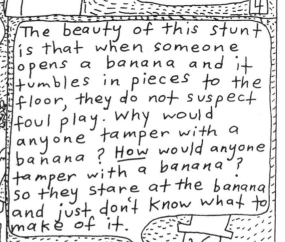

6

LARGE BLADDER STUNT

THIS WORKS BEST IF YOU CAN GO TO A BATHROOM WITHIN EARSHOT OF YOUR AUDIENCE.

HAVE A LARGE COOKING POT FILLED WITH WATER ALREADY IN THE BATHROOM.

GO INTO THE BATHROOM AND SHUT THE DOOR. NOISILY LIFT UP THE TOILET SEAT AND UNZIP YOUR TROUSERS.

BONK!! ZZZIP!

PICK UP YOUR POT OF WATER BY THE HANDLES AND GET A THIN STREAM OF WATER TRICKLING INTO THE TOILET.

AT FIRST NO ONE WILL NOTICE.

TRICKLE TRICKLE TRICKLE TINKLE

BUT AS THE STREAM CONTINUES UNABATED INTO THE SECOND MINUTE, IT WILL START TO SOUND VERY WRONG. YOU WILL CREATE A BEAUTIFULLY MADDENING TENSION IN YOUR LISTENERS.

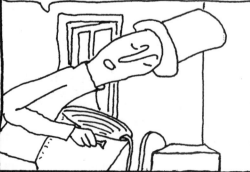

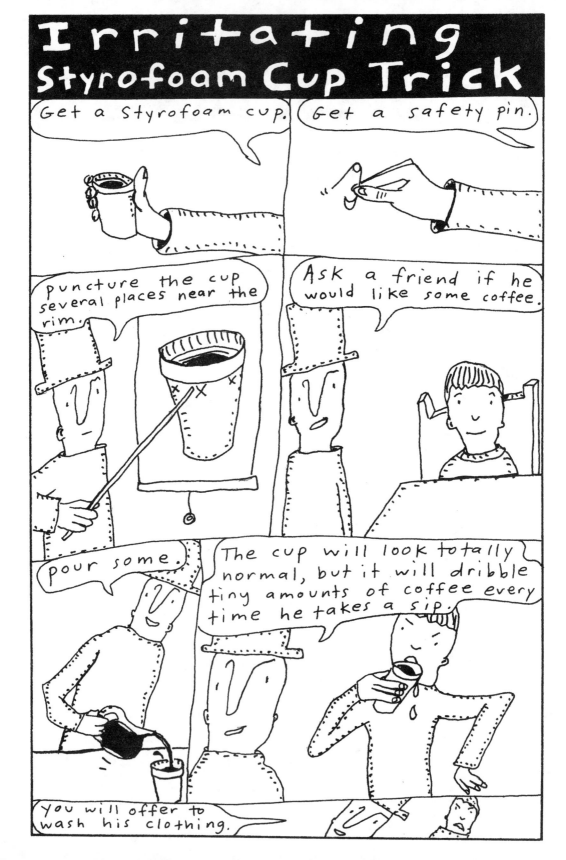

BELTLOOP POPPING

THIS IS A PARTICULARLY ELEGANT METHOD OF CONVINCING SOMEONE THAT YOU'VE JUST INTENTIONALLY YANKED OFF ONE OF THEIR BELTLOOPS.

START BY HOOKING YOUR INDEX FINGER INTO A PERSON'S BELTLOOP SO THE TIP OF THIS FINGER IS PUSHING OUT AGAINST THE INSIDE OF THE LOOP.

THEN PUSH THE INDEX FINGER THROUGH THE LOOPHOLE. THIS WILL MAKE A SNAPPING "THUD."

THE FRICTION AND THE SNAP OF THE FOLLOW-THROUGH WILL CAUSE AN UNCANNY SENSATION OF POPPED-BELTLOOPNESS.

COFFEE-SPILLING STUNT

You're having some people over for coffee.

Fill your cup with little pieces of paper instead of coffee.

Pretend to be sipping from your cup, blowing to cool it off, etc.

Then suddenly lose control of the cup and spill the paper onto someone.

Ahhhi

They will think temporarily that they might be able to sue you like the person who sued McDonald's.

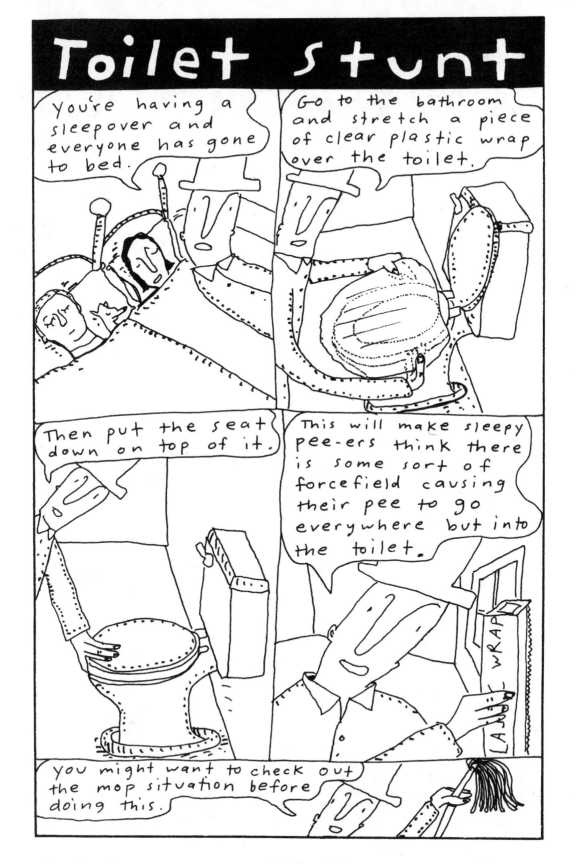

ADJUST-YOUR-NOSE-WITH-A-TABLE STUNT

Roller Shade Sabotage

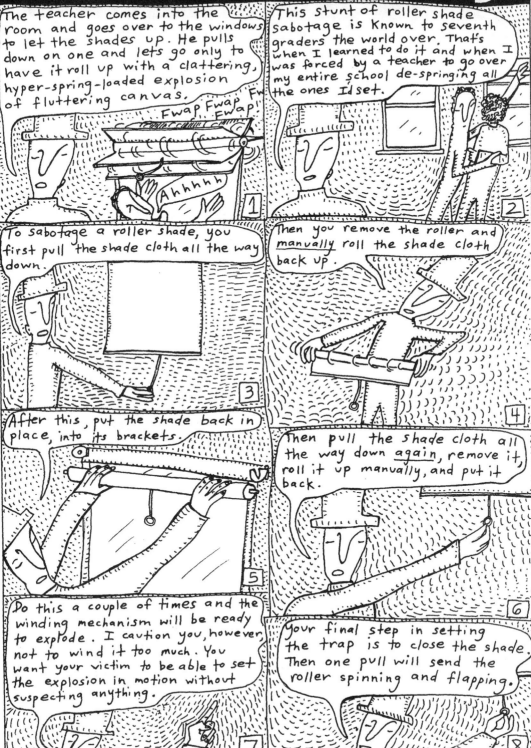

1. The teacher comes into the room and goes over to the windows to let the shades up. He pulls down on one and lets go only to have it roll up with a clattering, hyper-spring-loaded explosion of fluttering canvas. Fwap, Fwap, Fw... Fwap Ahhhhh

2. This stunt of roller shade sabotage is known to seventh graders the world over. That's when I learned to do it and when I was forced by a teacher to go over my entire school de-springing all the ones I set.

3. To sabotage a roller shade, you first pull the shade cloth all the way down.

4. Then you remove the roller and manually roll the shade cloth back up.

5. After this, put the shade back in place, into its brackets.

6. Then pull the shade cloth all the way down again, remove it, roll it up manually, and put it back.

7. Do this a couple of times and the winding mechanism will be ready to explode. I caution you, however, not to wind it too much. You want your victim to be able to set the explosion in motion without suspecting anything.

8. Your final step in setting the trap is to close the shade. Then one pull will send the roller spinning and flapping.

Hotel Trick

You will need the following: 1. a five dollar bill 2. a needle 3. black thread 4. a peep-hole in your door

First you sew the thread to the five dollar bill.

Then when the hotel hallway is clear,

Put the bill on the carpet and run the thread into your room.

Close the door.

Watch out the peep-hole as the passers-by examine the dropped money.

As soon as someone bends down to get it, you pull the bill back into your room.

FAKE-TASTING STUNT

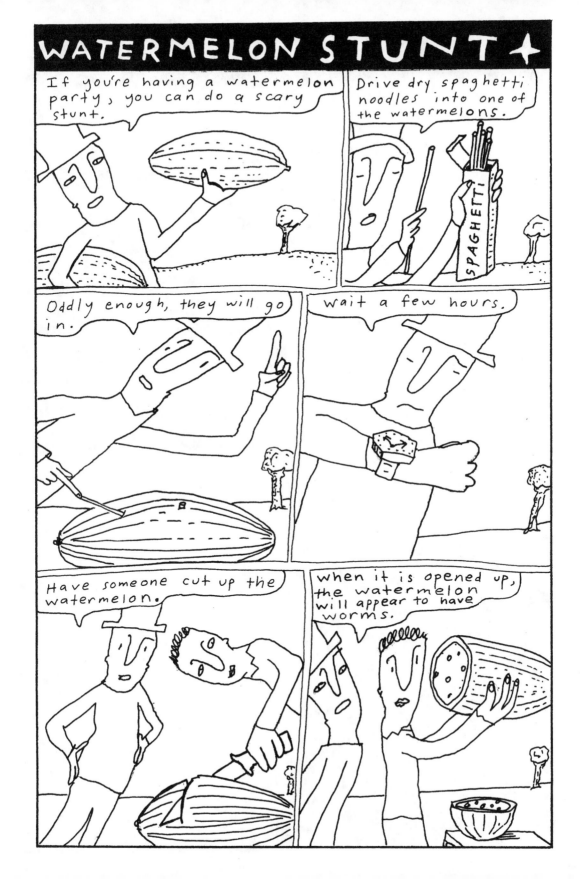

Game Show Stunt

This is a west-coast kind of stunt.

Have a friend who lives in a later time zone write down all the questions and answers to that night's episode of a game show.

Call them up and get the answers.

Study them.

Get together with some friends to watch the show and dazzle them with your brilliance.

What is a 200-pound mammal with fins, Alex.

HAT STUNT

IF YOU SEE A FRIEND OF YOURS BUYING A HAT,

SECRETLY BUY TWO IDENTICAL HATS, ONE 2 SIZES TOO SMALL, AND THE SECOND, 2 SIZES TOO LARGE.

PERIODICALLY SUBSTITUTE THE DIFFERENT HATS.

There is something *totally* wrong with that hat.

THIS WILL GIVE YOUR FRIEND THE ILLUSION THAT HIS HEAD IS ALTERNATELY EXPANDING AND SHRINKING.

Vacuum Cleaner Stunt

After a long drive I stayed the night at my friend Rob Hayes' house.

I'd arrived late and I was exhausted.

Just as I was drifting off to sleep, a vacuum cleaner started up in my room.

wheeeeeeeee

I turned on the light and searched the vacuum for an on/off switch. There wasn't one.

wheeeeee

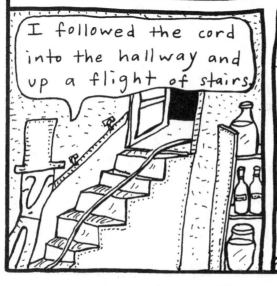

I followed the cord into the hallway and up a flight of stairs.

It went from there down another hallway and then under the door leading to Rob's bedroom.

He was in there, sniggering uncontrollably.

QUARTER STUNT

Have someone trace a quarter five times onto a piece of paper with a #2 pencil.

Then have them place their fingertips in the pattern and bear down hard for two ten-second periods.

After this, instruct them to take the quarter and attempt to steer it in a straight line -- like it's rolling -- from the top of their forehead and down their nose, using their two index fingers.

Explain that because of the minor stress you've created from bearing down, your right and left-handedness is temporarily altered. This makes it nearly impossible to make a straight line rolling the quarter.

The real stunt, of course, is that when you run the quarter across your face it makes a black trail from the graphite it collected while you traced it.

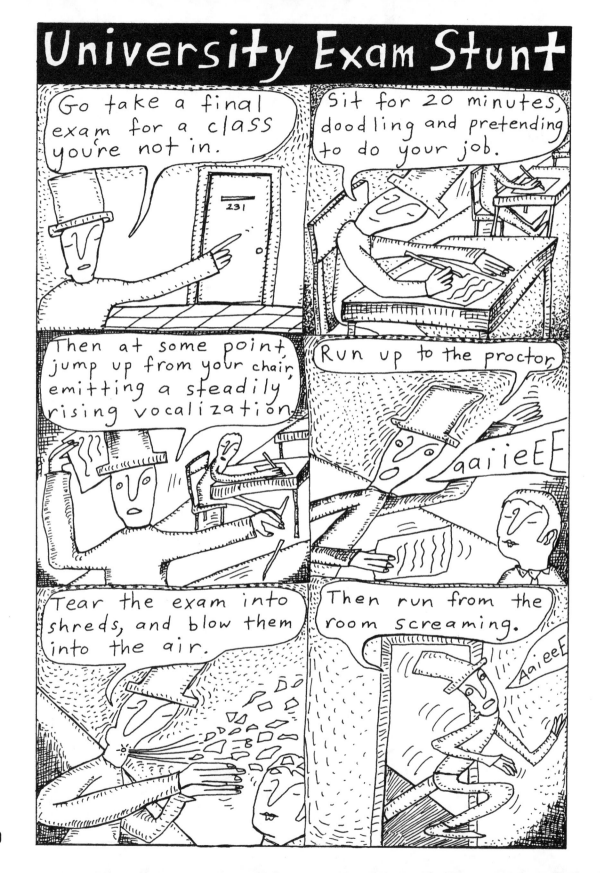

Scare The Passengers

when my friend Rob Hayes is driving, he waits for everyone to fall asleep.

Then he turns up the heat,

cold   hot   very hot

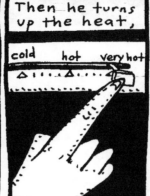

and the fan...

breezy   windy

full blast.

11.

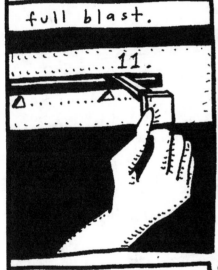

so everyone wakes up sweating and uncomfortably dazed.

when he has the passengers in this weakened state, he simultaneously turns off the headlights,

on
off

turns on the interior lights,

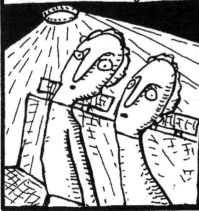

and opens all the windows,

se   open

while emitting a blood-curdling scream.

Aiiiiyarrri!

would I do this? No. But it made me laugh once·they took me off the defibrillator.

TOLL BOOTH STUNT

IF YOU'RE CARAVANING WITH ANOTHER CAR AND YOU COME TO A TOLL BOOTH,

PAY THE TOLL-BOOTH OPERATOR FOR YOURSELF AND YOUR FRIEND IN THE CAR BEHIND YOU.

THEN ASK THE TOLL-OPERATOR TO GIVE THE CAR BEHIND YOU A MESSAGE.

HEY, CURLY! THE CAR AHEAD OF YOU SAYS IT'S TIME TO START HAULING ASS.

SQUIRTING TOILET SEAT

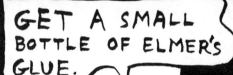

GET A SMALL BOTTLE OF ELMER'S GLUE.

REMOVE THE GLUE FROM THE BOTTLE AND FILL IT WITH WATER.

PLACE THE BOTTLE INCONSPICUOUSLY UNDER THE TOILET SEAT.

SO WHEN SOMEONE SITS ON THE SEAT THEY GET SQUIRTED BY A BLAST OF COLD WATER.

SPLASH!

FINGER-PULLING STUNT

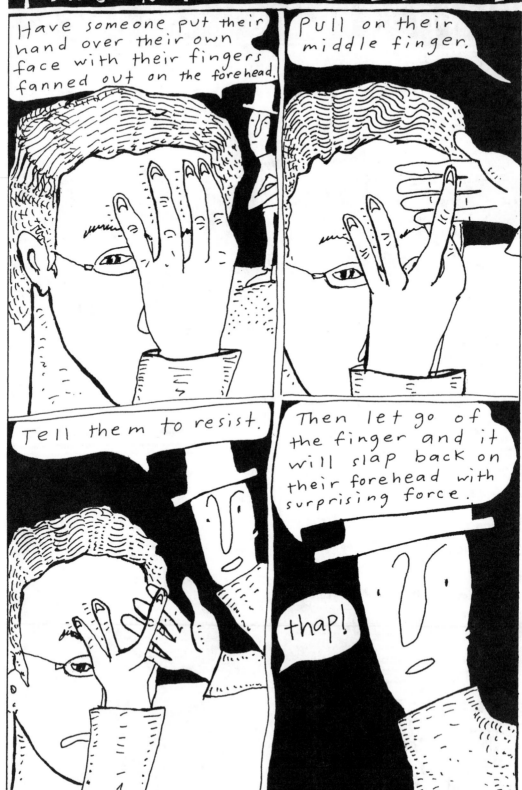

ATTACH-A-GLASS-OF-WATER-TO-THE-CEILING STUNT

You say to someone, "I can attach this glass of water to the ceiling using these three safety pins. Want to see me do it?"

you get up on a chair in the kitchen and you proceed with this seemingly impossible task.

At one point you drop one of your pins and say "could you get that?"

They reach over to get it and you empty your waterglass on them.

my mother did this trick to me more than once (believe it or not). To this day there is some part of me that thinks it actually is possible to pin a glass of water to the ceiling.

Scare the Driver

The driver is falling asleep at the wheel

You persuade him to take a nap in the passenger's seat while you drive.

Let him fall asleep for a few miles.

Then gently nudge him and ask: "Hey! Are you ok? I can drive. I can drive if you're sleepy. Hey! Let me drive."

ROOM REARRANGEMENT STUNT

This is a nice stunt if you're attending a weekend conference and you have access to a friend's room.

Wait until your friend is gone, then enter the room and take detailed notes on the exact location of everything in the space.

After this inventory, finally arrange the room. Line up his shoes, put socks in the dresser drawer lined up by color, make the bed so you can bounce a quarter on it, arrange shirts and pants, etc etc.

Your friend will come back, be totally surprised, laugh at the joke and so on. Then he'll eventually have to leave again.

Ha ha ha. OK, I gotta go.

He leaves. You re-arrange the room again. Just make it different. Switch pictures on the wall, move the bed, switch drawers for clothing. He'll come back again and he'll be like, "well...hell."

well, hell

You wait for him to leave again.

Oo... I'm late

Then you rearrange again, this time back to the original order (look at your notes.) mess up shirts, pants, unmake the bed, put stuff back in suitcase-- whatever.

This stunt causes the victim to feel as though he were in an episode of the Twilight Zone.

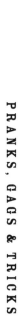

Lloyd's Fake Flat Tire

You will need duct tape and a piece of cardboard.

Go out to a friend's car.

Tape the cardboard to the tread of one of the tires.

When your friend drives away he will hear a "fwop...fwop...fwop" sound and think he has a flat tire.

vaseline Stunt

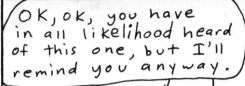

OK, ok, you have in all likelihood heard of this one, but I'll remind you anyway.

Grab the vaseline when everyone's gone to bed and slap a thin film of it onto the toilet seat.

This can potentially cause the blurry-eyed unsuspecting toilet-user (coming in at the wrong angle) to slide directly onto the floor.

At the very least, the sudden, tractionless sensation in the posterior will induce a feeling equal-parts rage and nausea.

That was not... funny.. I am not... AGGG!! Hurl... splash!

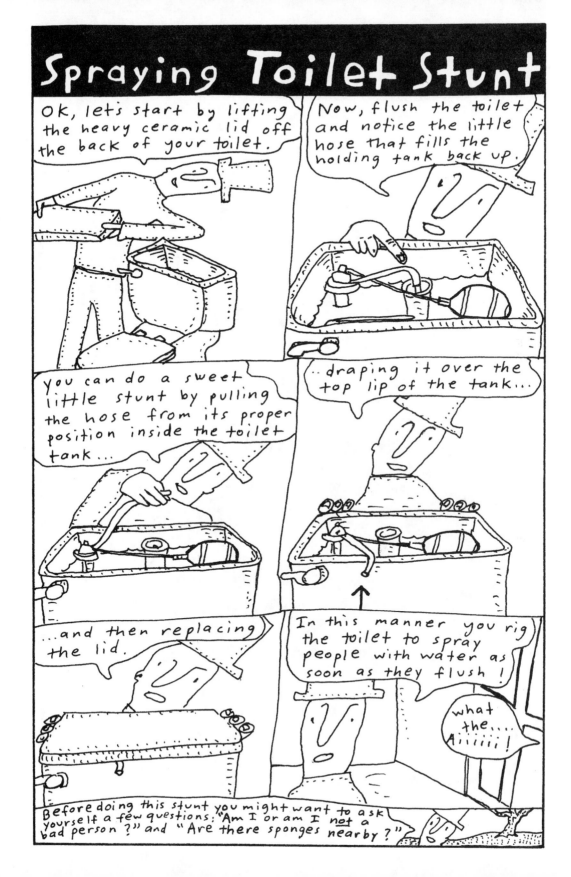

4 ODD SENSATIONS & GROSS-OUTS

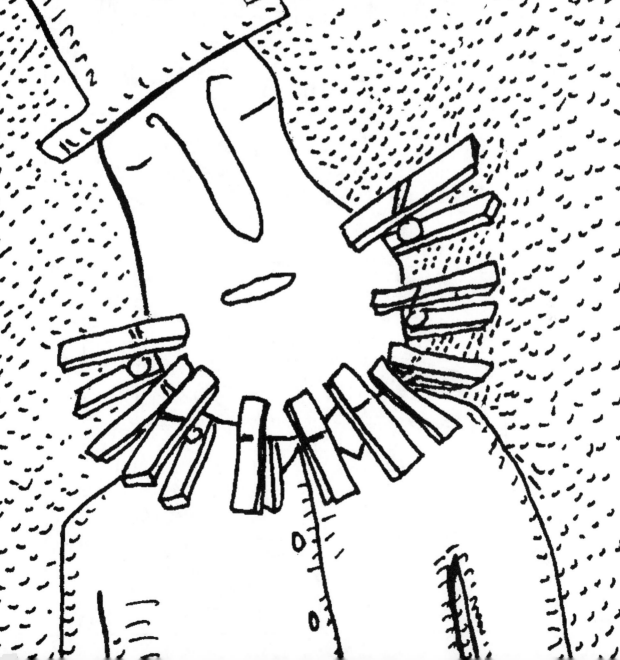

Clothespin Facial

1. This requires some element of pain tolerance.

2. Get about ten clothespins.

3. Attach them to the loose wattle of skin that forms your upper neck and lower jaw. There's a surprising amount of this skin.

4. If you succeed in attaching all ten clothespins, you'll have a surreal ruff of rigid jaw skin jutting out.

GOAT MOUTH

grasp your upper lip and lower lip with the respective fingers of your corresponding hands.

pull the lips apart.

extend tongue, making "mnahh" sound simultaneously. (the <u>only</u> sound you can make when holding on to both of your lips)

mnahh

"goat mouth" is an excellent alternative to clapping at boring concerts and board meetings.

Index Finger Snapping

This is one of the harder stunts to describe if you haven't already seen it.

Hold your thumb and middle finger together. Relax your index finger. (This a weird isolation but you'll get used to it.)

Next, raise your arm up

And then bring it down, snapping your wrist a little.

snap

This will cause the relaxed index finger to slap against the side of your middle finger.

When you get good at this, it can be really loud. Don't knock yourself out though. This technique is all finesse, not strength.

snap

Elbows

Did you know there are very few nerve endings in the skin of your elbows?

And that you can pinch or bite them quite hard without causing pain?

The person I learned this from, Nate Cooper, used to come up behind me,

gently bite onto my loose elbow skin,

and then give a persuasive pull with his teeth.

When I was little I would occasionally try to bite my own elbow.

It's impossible.

FINGER TOUCH + SWIVEL STUNT

WHILE STEERING YOUR CAR WITH YOUR WRISTS (MAYBE COME TO A STOP FIRST),

CONNECT RIGHT AND LEFT HAND FINGERTIPS, THUMB TO THUMB, INDEX TO INDEX, ETC. THIS IS HOME POSITION.

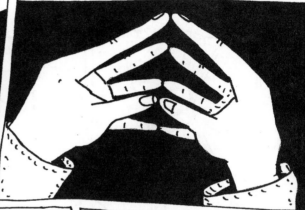

THEN: TURN HANDS CLOCKWISE ONE FINGER AND RE-CONNECT FINGERTIPS, SO, RIGHT THUMB TIP WILL TOUCH LEFT INDEX, RIGHT INDEX WILL TOUCH LEFT MIDDLE FINGER, ETC.

GO BACK TO HOME POSITION AND SWIVEL HANDS COUNTERCLOCKWISE ONE FINGER. RIGHT THUMB WILL TOUCH LEFT PINKY, RIGHT INDEX WILL TOUCH LEFT THUMB, AND SO ON.

THIS IS SURPRISINGLY DIFFICULT AND IT CREATES A MILD, DROOL-INDUCING NATURAL HIGH IF DONE FOR MORE THAN A FEW MINUTES.

THIS STUNT IS GOOD IN THE DARK.
COAT HANGER BRAIN GONG
GET SOME DENTAL FLOSS, A WIRE COAT HANGER, AND A METAL FORK.
DF
TIE A FOOT OR SO OF THE FLOSS ONTO EACH END OF THE HANGER.
WRAP THE OTHER ENDS OF THE FLOSS A COUPLE OF TIMES AROUND EACH INDEX FINGER, AND STICK YOUR INDEX FINGERS INTO YOUR EARS.
LET THE HANGER DANGLE IN THE AIR IN FRONT OF YOU AND HAVE SOMEONE GENTLY TAP THE HANGER WITH THE FORK.
IT WILL SOUND LIKE A GIANT GONG TO THE PERSON WITH THE DANGLING HANGER.
AND ABSOLUTELY NOTHING TO ANYBODY ELSE.

RiNG FiNGER STUNT

PLACE YOUR HAND ON A TABLE.

FOLD YOUR MIDDLE FINGER UNDER SO THE KNUCKLE RESTS FIRMLY AGAINST THE TABLE.

KEEPING THIS POSITION LIFT YOUR PINKY.

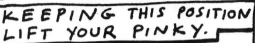

LIFT YOUR INDEX FINGER. TRY YOUR THUMB WHILE YOU'RE AT IT.

THEN, LIFT YOUR RING FINGER.

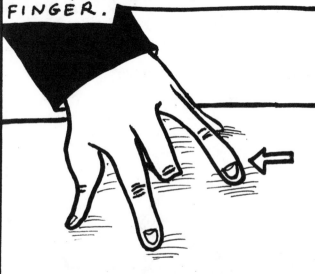

UNLESS YOU HAVE A RECENTLY INSTALLED BIONIC RING FINGER, IT WILL RESIST.

THEATER STUNT

THIS IS A STAGE WEIGHT. SOLID IRON AND QUITE HEAVY.

25 lbs.

THESE WEIGHTS ARE ALL OVER THE PLACE IN MOST THEATERS. IF YOU'RE EVER HANGING OUT BACKSTAGE, WAIT UNTIL ALL THE PERFORMERS HAVE LEFT THE DRESSING ROOM...

THEN PLACE TWO OR THREE STAGE WEIGHTS IN THE BOTTOM OF ONE OF THEIR BAGS.

IT IS A SHORT-LIVED STUNT BUT IT OFFERS AN AMAZING SENSATION FOR THE RECIPIENT.

OH MY GOD... I'M GETTING CHRONIC FATIGUE SYNDROME.

ARCTURAN WALKING STEP

IF YOU WANT TO BE PERCEIVED AS AN ALIEN BUT DON'T WANT TO PUT ON A FULL SET OF ANTENNAE OR WEIRD CONTACT LENSES, DO THE FOLLOWING:

AS YOU WALK, MOVE YOUR RIGHT ARM IN SYNC WITH YOUR RIGHT LEG, AND YOUR LEFT ARM IN SYNC WITH YOUR LEFT LEG.

YOU NORMALLY DO JUST THE OPPOSITE, AS YOU WILL FEEL AS SOON AS YOU TRY TO DO THIS FOR LONGER THAN ONE CITY BLOCK.

TRIANGLE SQUARE 12-COUNT DRAWING STUNT

HOLD YOUR INDEX FINGERS IN THE AIR ABOUT A FOOT APART.

STARTING IN THE UPPER LEFT SIDE OF AN IMAGINARY BOARD, SIMULTANEOUSLY DRAW A RIGHT TRIANGLE WITH YOUR RIGHT HAND AND A SQUARE WITH YOUR LEFT HAND.

KEEP DRAWING THESE FIGURES UNTIL YOU GET BOTH FINGERS BACK TO WHERE THEY BEGAN.

THIS WILL TAKE 12 COUNTS. COUNT ALOUD! (FOUR TRIANGLES FOR THE RIGHT AND THREE SQUARES FOR THE LEFT.)

HISSING FART SIMULATION

IF YOU HAVE ANY CANNED AIR LYING AROUND THE HOUSE (YOU KNOW, THAT STUFF YOU USE TO CLEAN OFF PHOTO AND COMPUTER EQUIPMENT?)--

PFSTT!

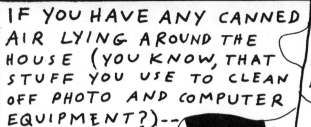

YOU CAN USE IT TO SIMULATE THE SOUND OF A SILENT-BUT-DEADLY FART.

YOU SIMPLY HANG OUT LOOKING UNCOMFORTABLE, SHIFTING FROM FOOT TO FOOT. THEN HIT THE SPRAY TOP AND LET OUT FOUR SOLID SECONDS OF HISSING.

FSSS SSS

THEN SNIFF A FEW TIMES, SAY "OUCH" AND WALK AWAY.

DON'T YOU FART ENOUGH AS IT IS WITHOUT HAVING TO SIMULATE ADDITIONAL FARTS?

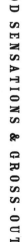

APPLE STUNT

THIS IS A TIME-CONSUMING STUNT BUT WELL WORTH IT.

GET AN APPLE, PREFER-ABLY AN OLDER ONE.

SQUEEZE AND SQUISH IT UNTIL THE GUTS OF THE FRUIT GET MUSHY.

BITE A SMALL HOLE IN THE SKIN. BE CAREFUL TO KEEP THE FLAP INTACT.

SUCK OUT THE INTERIOR OF THE APPLE,

THEN BLOW THE APPLE UP LIKE A LITTLE BALLOON AND HAND IT TO SOMEONE.

IT WILL DEFLATE IN THEIR HANDS AND INSPIRE IN THEM A STRANGE MIXTURE OF NAUSEA AND DISAPPOINTMENT.

pfft

Three Foot Snot Stunt

SALAMI STUNT

GET A SLICE OF SALAMI.

LICK IT.

PUT IT ON YOUR FOREHEAD.

ATTEMPT TO MOVE THE SALAMI INTO YOUR MOUTH SOLELY BY MANIPULATING FACIAL MUSCLES.

PANCAKE STUNT

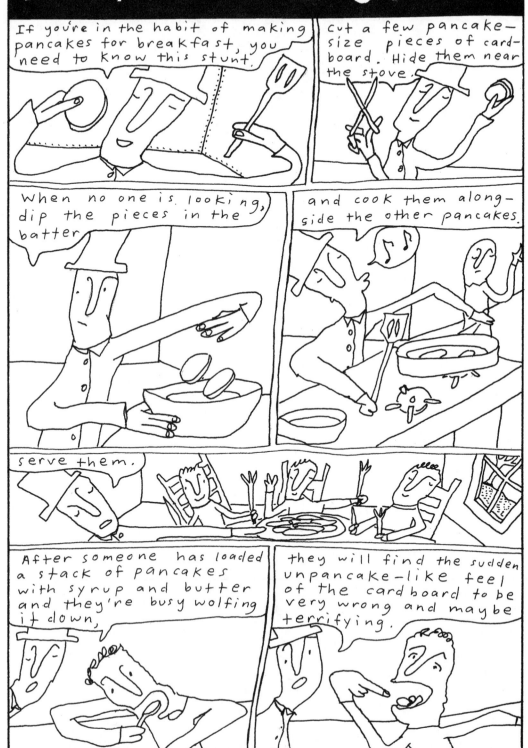

If you're in the habit of making pancakes for breakfast, you need to know this stunt.

cut a few pancake-size pieces of cardboard. Hide them near the stove.

When no one is looking, dip the pieces in the batter

and cook them alongside the other pancakes.

serve them.

After someone has loaded a stack of pancakes with syrup and butter and they're busy wolfing it down,

they will find the sudden unpancake-like feel of the cardboard to be very wrong and maybe terrifying.

IN-THE-EAR-AND-OUT-THE-MOUTH STUNT

CONCEAL A WADDED-UP NAPKIN IN YOUR MOUTH.

TAKE ANOTHER NAPKIN AND PRETEND TO STUFF IT INTO ONE OF YOUR EARS.

THEN SPIT THE CONCEALED NAPKIN OUT OF YOUR MOUTH.

NOTE CONCEALED NAPKIN

THIS GIVES THE PLEASANTLY IMPROBABLE ILLUSION THAT YOU'VE JUST PASSED A NAPKIN THROUGH YOUR BRAIN.

SPLATTERING HURL SIMULATION

THERE IS AN EASY WAY TO SIMULATE A SUDDEN DELUGE OF SPLASHING VOMIT.

BURP... KA-SPLASH!

YOU MUST HAVE A GLASS OF WATER.

THE TIMING OF IT IS EVERYTHING: YOU BURP, YOU WAIT FOR 1.5 SECONDS AND THEN YOU THROW THE WATER.

BAP

AND THEN, "UH-OH. HERE IT COMES AGAIN." SMACK LIPS 3 TIMES, BURP, WAIT, THROW THE WATER.

YOU NEED TO BE ABLE TO EMIT A CONTROLLED BURP. DO THIS BY SUCKING AIR INTO YOUR THROAT AND LETTING IT OUT.

HEEPF

BAP

YOU MUST HAVE A PLACE TO THROW THE WATER, LIKE A BATHTUB OR A SINK.

IT IS THE DELAY BETWEEN THE BURP AND THE SPLASH OF WATER THAT IS ACTUALLY THE GROSS THING.

SPLATTER

Fake Booger Stunt

1. Take a big glob of rubber cement and let it dry out on a piece of paper.

2. Scrape it off and roll it into a sticky little ball.

3. This will look more like a booger than you ever thought possible.

4. Then dangle it out of your nose and go up to someone and make a bit of conversation.

You know, I've never seen a field guide devoted to woodpeckers.

5. She will stare at your booger with a mounting horror, and then you will dislodge it, exclaiming "Hel-lo! Would you look at the size of this little fella."

This stunt does not play craftily along the subtle outer edge of disgusting; it plunges instead into the epicenter of the repulsive.

KETCHUP/COKE REVERSAL STUNT

Scenario: you're at a fast food "restaurant" with a friend. They have a coke or some other kind of soft drink. There is a little package of ketchup lingering innocently on the table. Your friend gets up to go to the bathroom.

As soon as he disappears, you flip the lid and the straw combo off the drink.

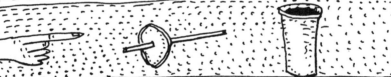

Then you make a little hole in the ketchup thingy and fit the ketchup package over the end of the straw-- the end that will go back into the coke.

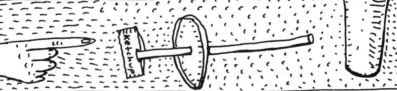

Do you follow me? Are you gagging? The next step naturally is to stick the straw with the ketchup on it **back** into the drink, and then wait for your friend to come back and take his first thirsty pull on the soft drink straw. You should be prepared to buy your friend a fresh drink, although this stunt done correctly will not contaminate the beverage. The stunt works nicely with milkshakes, I would imagine. I find this stunt exceptionally vile. but perfect.

BLOW-OUT-YOUR-BRAINS STUNT

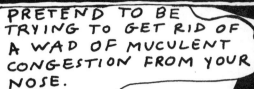

PRETEND TO BE TRYING TO GET RID OF A WAD OF MUCULENT CONGESTION FROM YOUR NOSE.

PFFFT! PFFT!

BLOW AND BLOW AND BLOW INTO A TISSUE OR A HANDKERCHIEF. SECRETLY FILL YOUR MOUTH WITH WATER.

THEN GIVE ONE TREMENDOUS FINAL BLOW WHILE SIMULTANEOUSLY SPITTING OUT THE ENTIRE MOUTHFUL OF WATER STRAIGHT OUT INTO THE HANDKERCHIEF.

PFFTT! BLAM!

IT WILL LOOK LIKE YOU'VE ACCIDENTALLY BLOWN YOUR BRAINS OUT YOUR NOSE.

FART-RECORDING STUNT

FOOD·CONCEALING STUNT

years ago I was eating lunch at a cafeteria with my friend, Sue Sternberg.

About halfway through the meal, Sue began giggling uncontrollably.

I ate my meal and with each bite, I saw her laugh more hysterically, until she was gasping for air.

"What?" I asked. "What? what? what?"

snig snig

she took what was left of a sandwich I'd been devouring, opened it up, and inside was the tail end of a banana peel.

She had concealed an entire banana peel in my sandwich as a joke, thinking I would notice it right away.

But instead I just proceeded to eat it like some hungry zoo animal, not noticing a thing.

zoo animal

187

SNEEZING STUNT

DIP YOUR FINGERS IN SOME WATER.

GO UP BEHIND SOMEONE AND PRETEND TO SNEEZE,

AHH.... CHOO!

AND THEN FLICK YOUR WET FINGERS AT THEIR NECK.

AHH-CHOO PFCH!

THAPP

THIS STUNT GIVES THE VICTIM THE AMAZING SENSATION OF BEING WETTED DOWN BY AN ENORMOUS SPRAY OF SALIVA LOADED WITH GERMS.

NASTY!

THE PEANUT BUTTER TOOTHPASTE TRICK

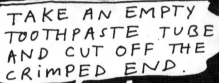

TAKE AN EMPTY TOOTHPASTE TUBE AND CUT OFF THE CRIMPED END.

FILL THE TUBE ABOUT HALF FULL WITH PEANUT BUTTER.

ye olde P.B.

FOLD THE END OVER ONCE AND STAPLE IT SHUT.

FOLD THE END SEVERAL MORE TIMES.

PLANT THE RIGGED TOOTHPASTE IN THE BATHROOM OF A FRIEND OR RELATIVE. WAIT.

LATER:

OH MY GOD! MOM! THE TOOTHPASTE HAS GONE BAD! IT'S TOTALLY BROWN!

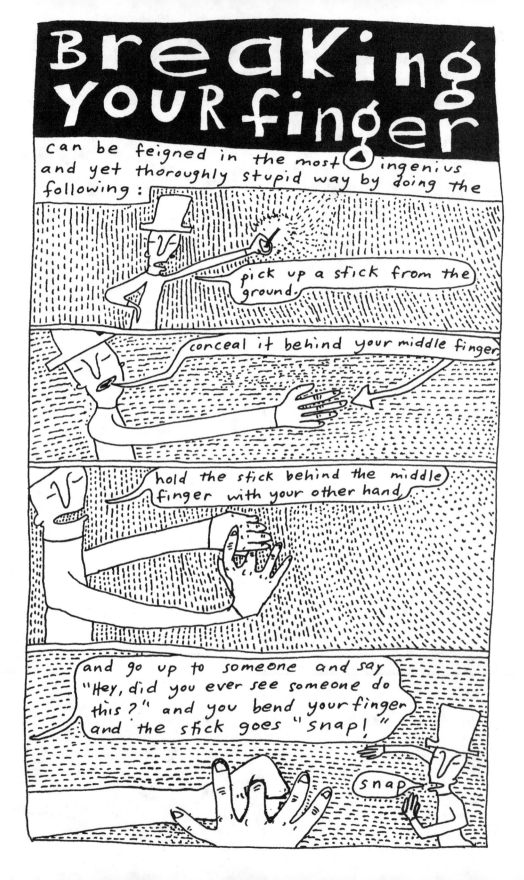

Have you felt my wart?

An alarming and yet easily executed stunt from my days as a preteen.

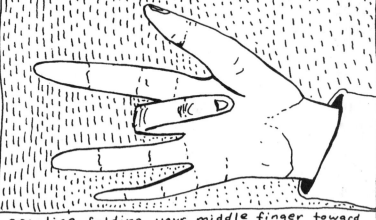

practice folding your middle finger toward your palm, as illustrated above. When you've got this down, go to someone and ask: "Have you felt my wart?" Don't wait for a response. (who wants to feel a wart?) Just go in for the kill: shake their hand with your middle finger folded over. It feels like you've got a wart the size of a guinea pig.

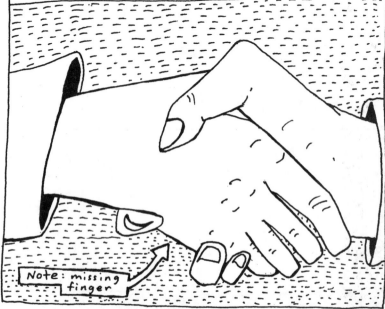

Note: missing finger

CHANGE-CHANNELS-WITH-YOUR-UVULA STUNT

A "UVULA" IS THAT LITTLE HANGY-DOWN THING IN THE BACK OF YOUR THROAT.

AMAZINGLY, YOU CAN USE IT TO CHANGE CHANNELS ON YOUR TV.

UVULA

SIMPLY FACE THE TV AND THEN POINT THE REMOTE INTO YOUR MOUTH AND CLICK THE CHANNEL-CHANGER.

THE SIGNAL WILL BOUNCE OUT YOUR MOUTH AND GO TO THE TV. CHANNELS WILL CHANGE.

SEEMS LIKE THERE'S A BIT OF MONEY TO BE WON WITH THIS STUNT. WOULDN'T YOU AGREE?

NO!

FINGER FOOD ✦

A guy came up to me in montana. He had a toothpick jabbed completely through his index finger.

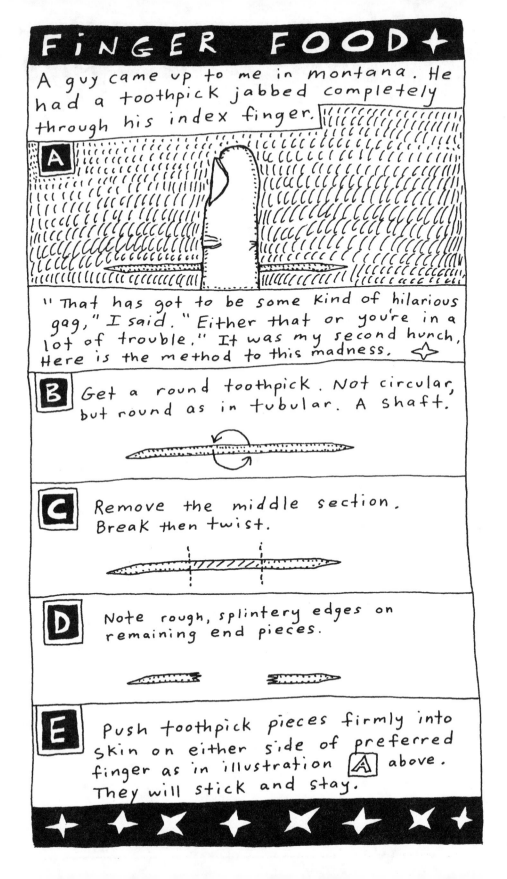

A

"That has got to be some kind of hilarious gag," I said. "Either that or you're in a lot of trouble." It was my second hunch. Here is the method to this madness. ✦

B Get a round toothpick. Not circular, but round as in tubular. A shaft.

C Remove the middle section. Break then twist.

D Note rough, splintery edges on remaining end pieces.

E Push toothpick pieces firmly into skin on either side of preferred finger as in illustration **A** above. They will stick and stay.

SUPERBALL BOOMERANG

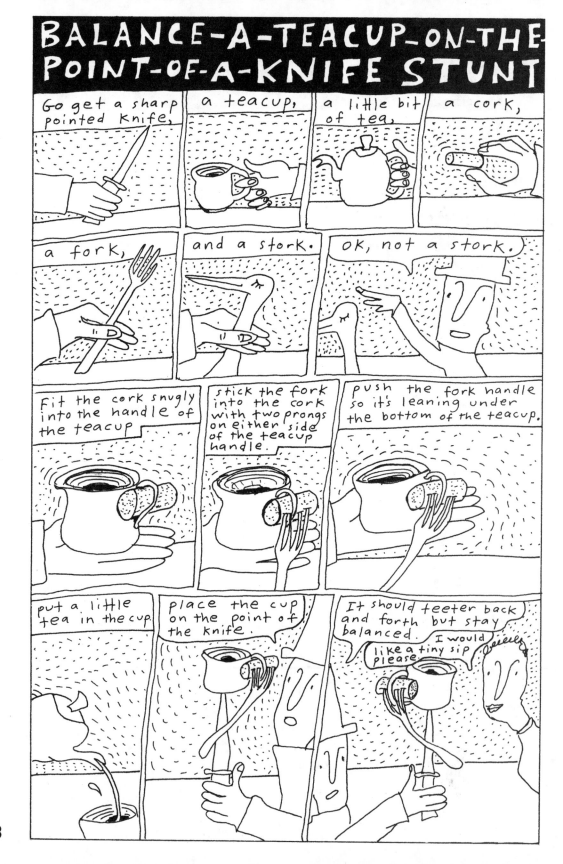

Mirror Writing

Get paper and a pen and go in front of a mirror.

Put the paper on your chest,

and then, watching the paper in the mirror, compose a letter to a friend.

writing like this is a little awkward, but persevere.

Look at your writing away from the mirror. It will be backward and indecipherable.

STRAW WRAPPER FLAPPER

DO THIS STUNT RIGHT AND IT WILL SOUND A BIT LIKE A SMALL MOTOR FROM FAR AWAY.

GET A STRAW WITH A PAPER WRAPPER. REMOVE ONE END OF THE WRAPPER.

PULL THE STRAW OUT OF THE WRAPPER ABOUT ONE INCH.

FLATTEN THE EXTRA PAPER FLAP.

HOLD THE STRAW AND HOLD THE FLAP. TEAR A HOLE IN THE STRAW WRAPPER BIG ENOUGH TO POKE THE STRAW THROUGH.

POKE THE STRAW THROUGH JUST A LITTLE BIT.

FOLD THE PAPER FLAP BACK AGAINST THE STRAW.

FOLD THE FLAP ITSELF IN HALF.

BEND THE WHOLE FLAP ASSEMBLY SO THE FLAP IS IN FRONT OF BUT NOT RESTING AGAINST THE STRAW OPENING.

SIDE VIEW

SUCK LIGHTLY ON THE OTHER END OF THE STRAW.

IF NOTHING HAPPENS, KEEP ADJUSTING THE FLAP DISTANCE AND ANGLE. KEEP SUCKING!

YOU'LL KNOW WHEN YOU GET IT RIGHT. THE FLAP STARTS PUTT-PUTTING.

THIS IS VERY SATISFYING.

French Fry Catapult

CRACKER-SPINNING STUNT

GET A SQUARE CRACKER. HOLD IT IN THE MIDDLE, BETWEEN YOUR THUMB AND INDEX FINGER. (OR BOTH INDEX FINGERS)

IF YOU BLOW ON ONE OF THE CORNERS OF THE CRACKER JUST RIGHT, YOU CAN MAKE THE CRACKER SPIN.

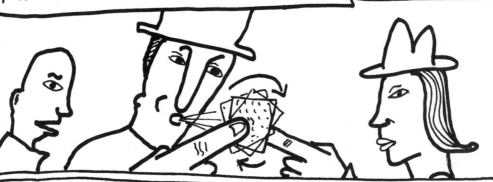

HOLD IT LOOSELY BUT NOT TOO LOOSELY. (OR IT MAY BLOW OUT OF YOUR HAND)

zzip!

ROLLING PENNY STUNT

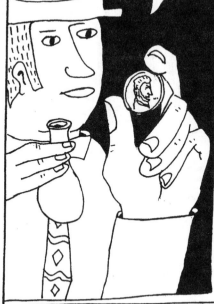

GET A PENNY AND A BALLOON.

STICK THE PENNY INSIDE THE BALLOON. BLOW THE BALLOON UP AND TIE A KNOT.

SHAKE THE BALLOON RHYTHMICALLY UP AND DOWN A COUPLE OF TIMES AND THEN HOLD IT STILL.

WITH A LITTLE PERSISTENCE YOU SHOULD BE ABLE TO MAKE THE PENNY ROLL REPEATEDLY AROUND THE INSIDE OF THE BALLOON ON ITS EDGE.

PING-PONG BALL BLOWING

GET A PING-PONG BALL. (AND WHILE YOU'RE AT IT, GET A TABLE, PADDLES, AND A NET. IT'S A FINE SPORT.)

TILT YOUR HEAD BACK AND HOLD THE BALL A FEW INCHES ABOVE YOUR MOUTH.

TAKE A HUGE BREATH AND BLOW AND THEN LET GO OF THE BALL. IT WILL FLOAT!

THIS IS NOT AN EASY STUNT, BUT PRACTICE IT AND YOU WILL DEVELOP A MIGHTY SET OF LUNGS.

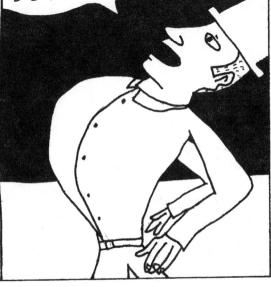

MAGIC FINGER STUNT

FILL A BOWL WITH WATER AND SHAKE PEPPER ONTO THE SURFACE

HAVE SOMEONE TEST THE WATER WITH THEIR FINGER. THEY'LL STICK IT IN AND NOTHING WILL HAPPEN.

THEN YOU CHANT A FEW MAGIC WORDS AND PUT YOUR FINGER INTO THE WATER.

(ON YOUR FINGER YOU'VE DABBED AN IMPERCEPTIBLE BIT OF LIQUID DETERGENT.)

AND VOILÁ! WATCH THE PEPPER SHOOT TO THE EDGES AND COWER THERE IN A DARK RING, LEAVING THE SURFACE OF THE WATER IMMACULATE.

HAIRDO SIMULATION

Have a friend with long hair lean her head backward so the hair swings out loosely in back.

This works nicely if you use the back of a chair for the person's neck.

Then the person who's going to get the hairdo puts her head under the cascade of hair and shapes it roughly onto her own head like a wig.

The audience is out in front and the only person who doesn't get to see the hairdo performance is the one donating her big hair.

USELESS TECHNIQUES

209

BANANA-BREAKING STUNT

IT IS POSSIBLE TO GRAB A BANANA AND YANK IT IN HALF

BUT IF YOU WERE TO PICK ONE UP AND TRY IT, WITHOUT THE PROPER TECHNIQUE, THE BANANA WOULD, IN ALL LIKELIHOOD NOT BREAK. (IT WOULD JUST END UP ELONGATED AND LEAKING.)

THE TRICK? HOLD IT IN FRONT OF YOU AND KEEP INDEX FINGERS SIDE BY SIDE. PULL AWAY EVER SO SLIGHTLY BUT MOSTLY PULL STRAIGHT OUT.

FOCUS AND THEN YANK.

snap!

ONCE YOU MASTER THIS STUNT, YOUR WORLD VIEW WILL SHIFT AND YOU WILL BE COMPELLED TO BREAK BANANAS UPON SIGHT FOR THE REST OF YOUR LIFE.

SHOVING PENCILS UP YOUR NOSE

You can simulate shoving a pencil into the deep recesses of your nose in the following manner:

Say to those who are watching--fellow 7th graders, churchgoers, what have you-- "I can shove this pencil into the farthest recesses of my nose."

Then show them the pencil <u>with your thumb on the eraser</u>

Hide the opening of your nose with two fingers

Then "shove," which is to say, <u>simulate</u> shoving. Remove your thumb from the eraser and move your hand over the pencil. <u>Do not move the pencil.</u>

make gagging and retching sounds as the pencil "goes in." Say, "oh my god ... I just touched ... my own ... brain with a pencil."

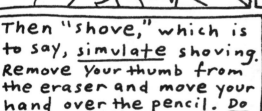

Then remove the pencil, clean it off on your shirt, and put it back in your pocket.

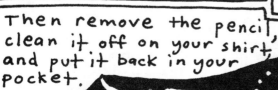

SNEEZING WITH FORK

STICK A FORK IN YOUR MOUTH.

HOLD A HANDKERCHIEF UP TO YOUR NOSE AND PRETEND TO SNEEZE.

WITH EACH SNEEZE BITE DOWN ON THE TINES OF THE FORK, CAUSING THE FORK TO LIFT THE HANDKERCHIEF.

THIS IS AN AMAZING PAIRING OF SOUND AND UNRELATED MOVEMENT. IT WORKS EQUALLY WELL WITH SNEEZING, COUGHING, AND NOSE-BLOWING.

FLYING NAPKIN STUNT

TILT YOUR HEAD BACK SO YOU'RE FACING THE CEILING.

PLACE AN UNFOLDED PAPER NAPKIN OVER YOUR FACE.

ON A COUNT OF THREE GIVE A MIGHTY BLOW AND SHOOT THE NAPKIN STRAIGHT INTO THE AIR.

SOMETIMES THE NAPKIN JUST STICKS TO YOUR FACE AND WON'T GO ANYWHERE,

BUT IT USUALLY FLIES UP TOWARD THE CEILING AND COMES GENTLY DOWN.

THIS IS GREAT DONE BY A LARGE GROUP AT A RESTAURANT TABLE.

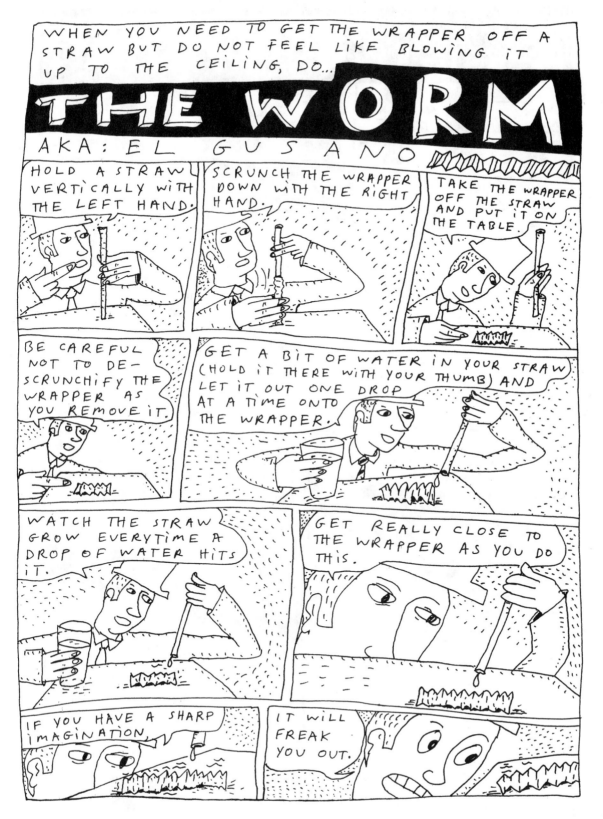

ANYA'S PENCIL-SPINNING STUNT

NOW <u>THIS</u> IS A STUNT! SPIN A PENCIL ONE TIME AROUND YOUR THUMB AND CATCH IT AGAIN.

THE TRICK? ANCHOR YOUR WRIST SO THE PINKY AND A COUPLE OF KNUCKLES ARE AGAINST A TABLETOP.

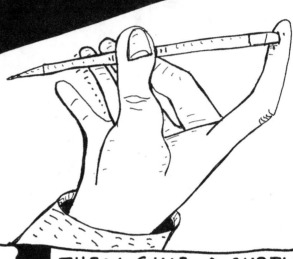

PUSH THE PENCIL FORWARD WITH YOUR INDEX FINGER,

THEN GIVE A SUBTLE SNAP WITH YOUR MIDDLE FINGER AND THIS WILL SPIN THE PENCIL AROUND AND INTO ITS ORIGINAL POSITION.

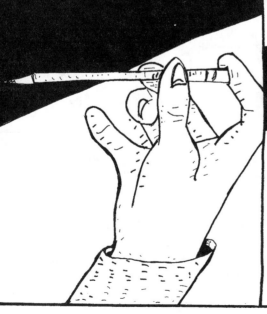

Fork, spoon, glass

A simple chain-reaction trick. Good at any restaurant or even at home.

you will need the following items:
1. A glass 2. A spoon 3. A fork

Next you will need to study the "Fork, spoon, glass" equation on chart F.

Chart F

Most will agree that the equation on chart "F" can be summarized as follows: you whomp on the pointy end of the fork, which causes the spoon to fly into the air.

what you try to do is: get that spoon into the glass.

NAME-WRITING STUNT

IT IS POSSIBLE TO WRITE YOUR NAME BACKWARD AND FORWARD AT THE SAME TIME.

HOLD A PEN IN EACH HAND.

WRITE THE FIRST LETTER OF YOUR NAME FORWARD WITH YOUR RIGHT HAND AND BACKWARD WITH YOUR LEFT.

THE RIGHT HAND KNOWS WHAT TO DO. THE LEFT HAND COPIES IN A MIRROR-IMAGE.

WRITE THE REST OF YOUR NAME. DON'T THINK TOO MUCH.

NOTE: IF YOU ARE LEFT-HANDED, YOU WILL WRITE YOUR BACKWARD AND FORWARD NAMES SO THEY'RE COMING TOWARD EACH OTHER, NOT GOING APART.

Styrofoam cup trick

get a styrofoam cup.

push a little hole in the bottom of it with your thumbnail.

smoosh your nose into the hole in the bottom of the cup. The styrofoam will tighten around your nose and the cup will stay there protruding.

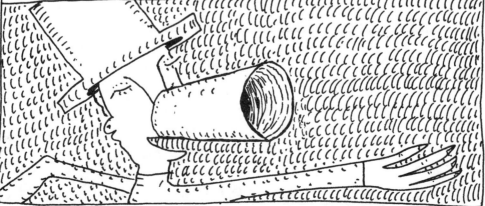

STUNT
face-slapping

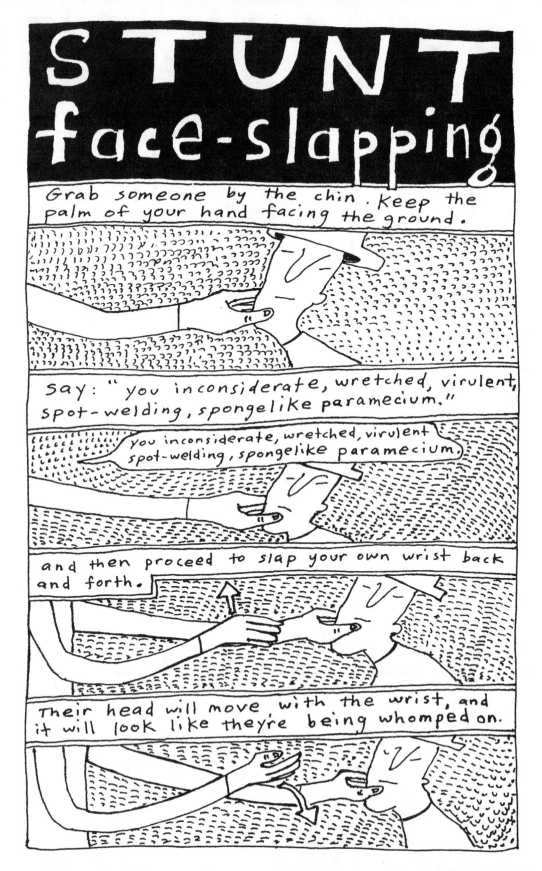

Grab someone by the chin. Keep the palm of your hand facing the ground.

Say: "you inconsiderate, wretched, virulent, spot-welding, spongelike paramecium."

you inconsiderate, wretched, virulent spot-welding, spongelike paramecium.

and then proceed to slap your own wrist back and forth.

Their head will move with the wrist, and it will look like they're being whomped on.

Sideways Spitting

I saw my friend Jimmy Leary invent and perfect this when we were eight.

It evolved naturally enough from regular spitting, which we were doing quite a lot of.

Regular spitting: straight out of the mouth.

..and then spitting.

Sideways spitting simply involves moving the spitting orifice to one side of the mouth...

The advantage of sideways spitting for Jimmy as I recall was that he could be having a conversation face to face with someone and spit without moving his head away from the person he was talking to.

Because of obvious risks involved with sideways spitting, I suggest you practice the following:

place your hand in front of your mouth, shift spitting orifice to one side, and blow air.

you shouldn't feel the blowing on your hand. when you're good at blowing, move to spitting.

NOSE CRACKING

SAY TO SOMEONE:

DID YOU KNOW YOU CAN CRACK YOUR NOSE JUST LIKE YOU CRACK YOUR KNUCKLES?

CRACKLE CRUNCH

COVER YOUR NOSE WITH YOUR HANDS.

HOOK A THUMBNAIL BEHIND YOUR FRONT TEETH. PULL THE NAIL OVER A TOOTH. THIS WILL MAKE A CRACKING SOUND.

DO THIS WHILE SIMULTANEOUSLY MOVING YOUR NOSE WITH YOUR FINGERS.

KNUDD KNUDD KNUDD

WHEN PEOPLE SEE MOVEMENT ACCOMPANIED BY NOISE, THEY ASSUME THEY'RE CONNECTED.

NOSE CRACKING PART 2

IF YOU SHOW SOMEONE THE NOSE CRACKING STUNT, THEY MAY VERY WELL KNOW IT. IT'S BEEN AROUND FOR AWHILE. HOWEVER, THEY MIGHT NOT KNOW THIS VARIATION.

SAY: I CAN CRACK MY NOSE.

YEAH, RIGHT. YOU HOOK YOUR THUMB BEHIND YOUR TOOTH. HA HA.

SNIK SNIK

YOU SAY:

NO. I REALLY CRACK MY NOSE. NO GIMMICKS. NO THUMBNAILS. I HAVE VERY LOOSE AND CRUNCHY NOSE CARTILAGE.

OK... LET'S HEAR SOME CRUNCH-ING.

YOU SAY, "HANG ON A SECOND. I HAVE TO TIE MY SHOES." BEND DOWN AND SLIP A PIECE OF DRY, UNCOOKED PASTA INTO YOUR MOUTH.

NOTE: SHOES HAVE NO LACES WHATSOEVER.

GET UP AND SAY, "LOOK," AND THEN PUSH ON YOUR NOSE WITH YOUR INDEX FINGERS. AS YOU PUSH, BITE DOWN ON THE DRY PASTA.

CRACK...CRACK CRACK.

WHEN THE PERSON IS NOT LOOK-ING SPIT OUT THE PASTA. OR SWALLOW IT.

YECHH

USELESS TECHNIQUES

DRY STRAW WHISTLE

PINCH ONE END OF A STRAW WITH THE INDEX FINGER AND THUMB OF BOTH HANDS.

BLOW ACROSS THE TOP OF THE STRAW

WHILE SLIDING (BUT STILL PINCHING) YOUR RIGHT HAND TO THE TOP OF THE STRAW, YOUR LEFT HAND STAYS AT THE BOTTOM, STILL PINCHING THE STRAW CLOSED.

BZZHHW

BLOW AS YOU SQUEEZE OUT A SHRINKING COLUMN OF AIR. THE SOUND PRODUCED WILL BE QUIET BUT EERIE.

JUMPING CUP

GET A COUPLE OF PAPER CUPS.*

* OR PLASTIC

STACK THEM ONE INSIDE THE OTHER. HOLD ONTO THE BOTTOM ONE.

BLOW AT THE CUP RIMS AT ABOUT A 45° ANGLE.

IF YOU GET THE ANGLE RIGHT AND THE PROPER BREATH VELOCITY, THE TOP CUP WILL FLY UP INTO THE AIR.

USELESS TECHNIQUES

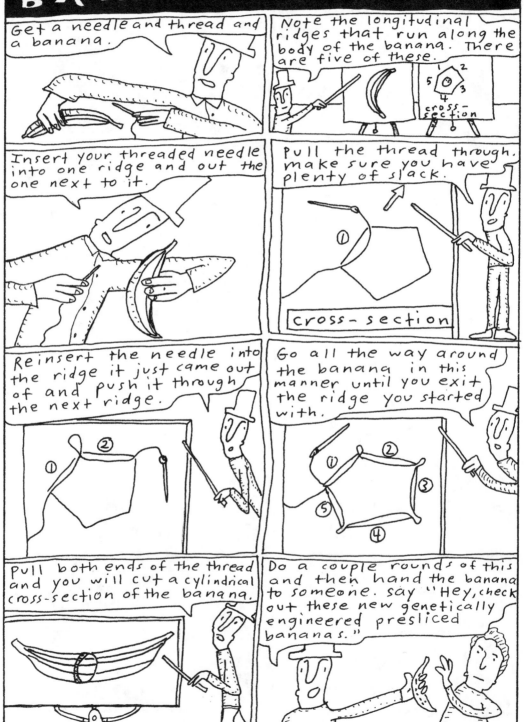

Plant Missiles

once you figure out how to make a plant missile and you can easily identify the plant to do it with, you will be programmed to make the missiles for the rest of your life.

This is what you use:

European Plantain

The plants grow near sidewalks everywhere. They have a long, sharp-edged stalk with a little, missile-shaped head on top. Their leaves fan out at the bottom.

To shoot your own plant-missile you simply pluck up one of the stalks and hold it with your left hand.

Then take the flexible bottom part in the other hand and loop it around the top of the stalk, below the tip.

Tighten this loop and pull it up against the head.

When you're ready, you point your plant and pull the head off the stalk.

Because of the structure of this plant, the head flies off the stalk and goes really far, usually between six and eight feet.

STRAW POPPING

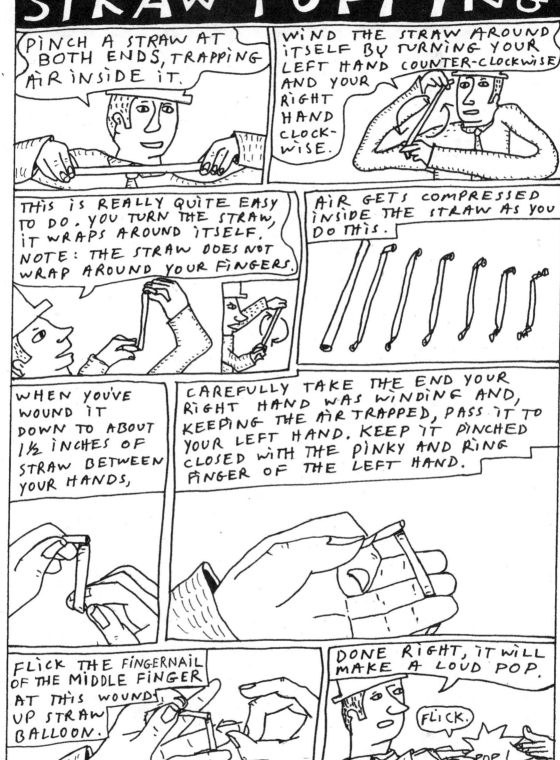

PINCH A STRAW AT BOTH ENDS, TRAPPING AIR INSIDE IT.

WIND THE STRAW AROUND ITSELF BY TURNING YOUR LEFT HAND COUNTER-CLOCKWISE AND YOUR RIGHT HAND CLOCK-WISE.

THIS IS REALLY QUITE EASY TO DO. YOU TURN THE STRAW, IT WRAPS AROUND ITSELF. NOTE: THE STRAW DOES NOT WRAP AROUND YOUR FINGERS.

AIR GETS COMPRESSED INSIDE THE STRAW AS YOU DO THIS.

WHEN YOU'VE WOUND IT DOWN TO ABOUT 1½ INCHES OF STRAW BETWEEN YOUR HANDS,

CAREFULLY TAKE THE END YOUR RIGHT HAND WAS WINDING AND, KEEPING THE AIR TRAPPED, PASS IT TO YOUR LEFT HAND. KEEP IT PINCHED CLOSED WITH THE PINKY AND RING FINGER OF THE LEFT HAND.

FLICK THE FINGERNAIL OF THE MIDDLE FINGER AT THIS WOUND UP STRAW BALLOON.

DONE RIGHT, IT WILL MAKE A LOUD POP.

FLICK.

POP!

The whistled "S"

Sˢeven Sˢturgeons were celebrating, uh, I mean, cˢelebrating their sˢecond sˢabbatical.

You've heard of "rolling your 'R's" I would assume. (And if you can't do it, try this trick: say: "ada" over and over again; this will propel your mouth into a rolled "r" the same way the pull-cord starts up the lawnmower.)

ada..ada..ada..ada..adadadadarrrrrr

Let's move on to the whistled "s." Like the rolled "r," this is a nice, somewhat musical, embellishment you can add to everyday conversation. The basic idea is: whenever you have an "s" sound, whether from an "s" or a "c," you are already extremely close to whistling. So, instead of holding back or stifling the whistle, you lean in to the whistle that lurks potentially in _every_ "s" sound and force it out. "Shazam" becomes "sˢhazam."

excˢuse me. I would like to buy a sˢnake. On second thought... sˢecond thought... make that a ada..ada..ada.... adadadarrrrrrrrodent.

A volley of whistled "S'es will add life to any routine exchange of pleasantries, as will the unpredictably rolled "r."

NEWFOUNDLAND MUMMER'S LANGUAGE

AROUND CHRISTMASTIME IN NEWFOUNDLAND, SOME PEOPLE GO MUMMING FROM HOUSE TO HOUSE.

THEY WEAR DISGUISES SO NO ONE CAN RECOGNIZE THEM AND THEY PUT ON SMALL PERFORMANCES IN EXCHANGE FOR FOOD AND DRINK.

TO INSURE NO ONE KNOWS WHO THEY ARE, THEY ALSO DISGUISE THEIR VOICES: THEY TALK WHILE INHALING RATHER THAN WHILE EXHALING.

CAN YOU UNDERSTAND?

air

YOU TOO CAN DO THIS. DON'T INHALE TOO HARD OR IT WILL MAKE YOU COUGH.

→ THE WORDS GO ALL THE WAY IN

DO IT SOFTLY AND YOUR VOICE WILL TAKE ON AN EERIE VIBRATION, REMINISCENT OF A PIECE OF PAPER HITTING THE BLADES OF AN ELECTRIC FAN

BING CROSBY LANGUAGE

IF YOU ARE KILLING TIME WITH SOMEONE YOU KNOW QUITE WELL YOU MIGHT TRY COMMUNICATING WITH EACH OTHER IN THE VERY FRUSTRATING BING CROSBY LANGUAGE.

Ying

"I WOULD LIKE TO GO TO THE ZOO," TRANSLATES AS:

I WING LOSBY TING GOSBY TING TOSBY

SHORT WORDS STARTING WITH VOWELS STAY AS THEY ARE (I, AM, ARE, IT, OUT etc.). ALL OTHER WORDS KEEP THEIR FIRST LETTER BUT HAVE THE BODY OF THE WORD REPLACED BY AN ALTERNATING PATTERN OF -ING AND -OSBY.

short words =
sh-ing w-osby

BECAUSE OF THE IN-COMPREHENSIBLE NATURE OF BING CROSBY LANGUAGE, IT SHOULD NEVER BE USED IN EMERGENCY SITUATIONS.

TING A BOSBY! WING OUT!! *

* THERE'S A BEAR! WATCH OUT!!

IN-OUT LANGUAGE

A cross be- -tween talk -ing and breath -ing

This stunt language is directly linked to "Eeffin'," so you might want to read up on that while you're at it.

I (inhale)

would (exhale)

LIKE (inhale)

to (exhale)

BUY (inhale)

a (exhale)

NEWS- (inhale)

pap- (exhale)

-ER (inhale)

OK

This is just like normal talking, except instead of talking while just exhaling, which is normally what you do when talking, you alternately inhale and exhale on each syllable. This resembles "eefin'," but it replaces "eefin's" "Bum-titty" with a rhythm more like that of the polka. Use your diaphragm.

ABSURD LANGUAGES & MOUTH ACTIVITIES

241

dog-snorting

abstract: an exhalation followed by a sudden, forced inhalation through the mouth produces a highly favorable sound.

1 First you must "ruff" like a dog. Do this ten times. Right now.

> ruff...ruff..ruff..ruf

2 Now practice snorting. This is done by inhaling suddenly.

> snngkk...snngk...snort..

3 At this point, go back to your exhaled "ruff," following it with a sudden pull-back of air. Think "snorting sound."

snorting sound → -V/

> ruff...sngkrt

4 If you are making a "ruff" followed immediately by a percussive snort, you are dog-snorting.

> ruff-snort

> congratulations

5 If you are having trouble getting a good dog-snort, try doing a succession of three. Sometimes this builds a certain momentum and snort quality improves.

> ruffsnort ... ruffsnort.. ruffsnort

DO-iT-YOURSELF WATER FOUNTAIN STUNT

FILL A GLASS HALF FULL OF WATER (OR HALF EMPTY DEPENDING ON HOW YOU'RE FEELING).

PUT A STRAW IN IT.

MASH YOUR MOUTH AGAINST THE TOP OF THE GLASS AND MAKE A TIGHT SEAL. BLOW.

WATER WILL GUSH OUT THE STRAW AND DRENCH WHOEVER IS SITTING NEXT TO YOU.

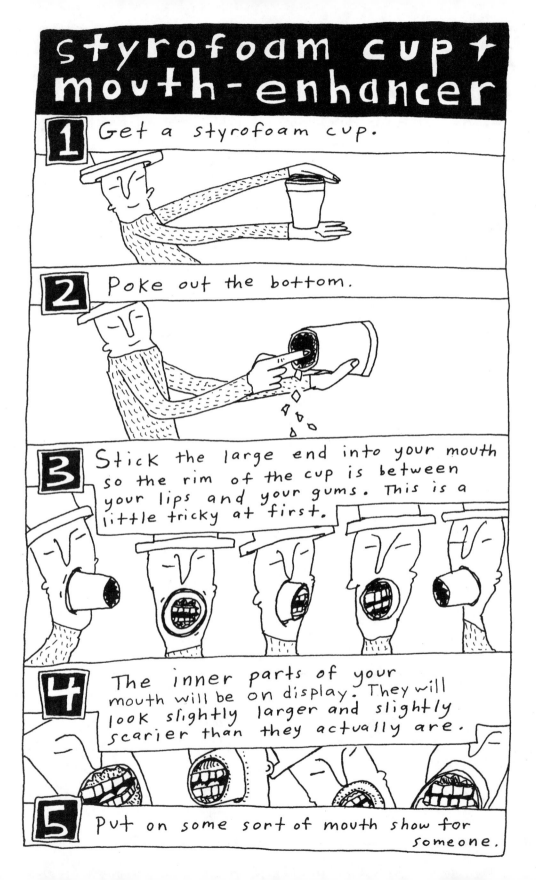

styrofoam cup + mouth-enhancer

1 Get a styrofoam cup.

2 Poke out the bottom.

3 Stick the large end into your mouth so the rim of the cup is between your lips and your gums. This is a little tricky at first.

4 The inner parts of your mouth will be on display. They will look slightly larger and slightly scarier than they actually are.

5 Put on some sort of mouth show for someone.

HOW TO EAT LIKE A LiZARD STUNT

HOLD A PIECE OF LETTUCE IN FRONT OF YOUR FACE.

PAUSE AND THEN LURCH, GRABBING THE LETTUCE WITH YOUR MOUTH

LEAVE MOST OF IT HANGING OUTSIDE YOUR CLOSED LIPS.

BITE UP ON THE LETTUCE TAKING MORE OF IT INTO YOUR MOUTH. DO THIS A FEW TIMES, PAUSING BETWEEN BITES. NOTE: MOVE ONLY THE TOP PART OF YOUR JAW WHEN DOING THIS.

FINALLY, TILT YOUR HEAD BACK AND BITE PERCUSSIVELY UNTIL THE LETTUCE DISAPPEARS.

GAK
GAK
GAK
GAK

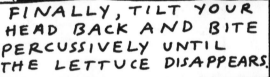

Laughing without Smiling

even creepier than it sounds.

ah heh heh heh
ah heh heh heh

ho ho ho ho ho
ho ho ho ho ho ho ho h ho ho.

start slow with your chosen affected laugh sound and then speed it up. Keep your jaw loose. No smiling.

ee hee ee hee
ee hee ee hee eehee.

it is impossible, of course, for this not to evolve into real laughter.

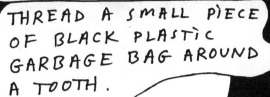

MISSING TEETH

THREAD A SMALL PIECE OF BLACK PLASTIC GARBAGE BAG AROUND A TOOTH.

CUT OFF THE EXCESS. DON'T CUT YOUR TONGUE!

THIS IS UNCOMFORTABLE BUT PLEASANTLY REALISTIC.

WOW. YOU TOTALLY LOOK LIKE A HOCKEY PLAYER.

Leaf Bombarde

whheeee

a bombarde is an instrument found in Breton music. It is kind of like those instruments snake charmers use, loud and reedy.

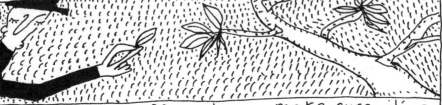

Grab a leaf off a tree. make sure it's a nice mouth-sized leaf, preferably roundish. make sure you're grabbing from a tree and not an oversized poison ivy bush. make sure it is a leaf and not a large flat insect.

ok already

put the leaf on your tongue and press it against the roof of your mouth.

Blow.

wheeeeee

you'll have to fool around with the leaf's position as well as your gag-reflex, if you're at all like me. when the noise finally comes out it will be high-pitched and kazooish and to say the least, rather irritating. ✩✩✩✩ ✩✩✩

THE ZURNA

A MERCILESSLY LOUD NOISE-MAKING DEVICE.

ALL YOU NEED TO MAKE ONE IS A STRAW AND A PAIR OF SCISSORS.

BITE ONE END OF THE STRAW SEVEN TIMES TO FLATTEN IT A BIT.

WITH THE SCISSORS CUT A POINT ON THE FLATTENED END OF THE STRAW.

CLOSE UP

BITE IT SEVEN MORE TIMES.

STICK THE POINTY END OF THE STRAW INTO YOUR MOUTH ABOUT 1/2 AN INCH AND BLOW HARD.

DONE CORRECTLY THE PART YOU CUT WILL TURN INTO A DOUBLE REED AND PEOPLE WILL DEMAND THAT YOU "STOP MAKING THAT NOISE!"

ZWEEEE

WHAT IS BETTER THAN ONE ZURNA?

TWO ZURNAS!

HOW MANY CAN YOU BLOW AT ONCE?

ZURNA SCALE

IF YOU MASTER THE STRAW ZURNA, PEOPLE WILL EVENTUALLY COMPLAIN.

THIS IS YOUR CUE TO TAKE THE INSTRUMENT TO THE NEXT LEVEL.

BLEEEEEF

IT'S NOT VERY... UH... "MUSICAL," REALLY.

HEY, I CAN PLAY A SCALE ON MY ZURNA JUST LIKE YOU PLAY ONE ON A HAMMOND ORGAN, JACK!

GET SOME SCISSORS AND TAKE A HUGE LUNG OF AIR.

START BLOWING THE ZURNA AND THEN CUT OFF A PIECE OF IT ABOUT 3/4 OF AN INCH LONG.

DO,.. RE.

CONTINUE CUTTING PIECES AND TRAVELLING UP THE SCALE.

LA. TI...

mi, FA,.SOL

UNTIL YOU HIT THE NOTE AN OCTAVE ABOVE THE NOTE YOU STARTED WITH.

DO♪

YOU'LL HAVE TO ADJUST YOUR PITCH BY BLOWING SOFTER OR HARDER WITH EACH CUT.

YOUR AUDIENCE WILL INEVITABLY SAY:

OK, THAT'S GREAT. NOW GO BACK DOWN THE SCALE.

YOU SAY:

HEY, BLAH BLAH BLAH! I WIN.

WHEE EE EE

ventriloquism at tollbooths

Requires: one person hidden behind the driver's seat and another person (the driver) who will mouth the words.

Also: you'll need an audience in the rest of the vehicle to watch the performance.

so, you've pulled up to the tollbooth and the tollbooth operator says:

That'll be a dollar fifty ma'am.

and you the driver begin moving your lips while the hidden "ventriloquist" says:

How do I get to the nearest diner? Thank you for your help. Have a good day.

TRAPDOOR SQUIRTING STRAW STUNT

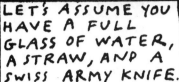

LET'S ASSUME YOU HAVE A FULL GLASS OF WATER, A STRAW, AND A SWISS ARMY KNIFE.

CUT A LITTLE HOLE IN THE SIDE OF THE STRAW ABOUT ONE INCH FROM THE END. IT'S A SECRET HOLE SO DON'T GO CALLING ATTENTION TO IT.

PUT THE STRAW INTO THE WATER GLASS AND DRINK.

THEN, NONCHALANTLY PINCH THE SUBMERGED END OF THE STRAW AND RAISE THE SECRET HOLE SO IT IS ABOVE THE LEVEL OF THE WATER.

AIM AND BLOW. YOU'LL HAVE A CRUDE BUT EFFECTIVE SQUIRTING DEVICE.

from Mark Conkle
S. BARTLETT

EXPOSED TEETH TRICK

TAKE THE CORNER OF YOUR SHIRT...

AND WITH IT, SWAB OUT ALL THE SALIVA BETWEEN YOUR UPPER LIP AND TOP ROW OF TEETH.

THEN PUSH YOUR TOP LIP UPWARDS. THE SUDDEN DRYNESS YOU'VE CREATED WILL MAKE IT STICK THERE...

EXPOSING YOUR TOP FRONT ROW OF TEETH IN A CREEPY AND UNNATURAL MANNER.

THE BEST OF STUNTOLOGY

258

DiDGERi-DON'T

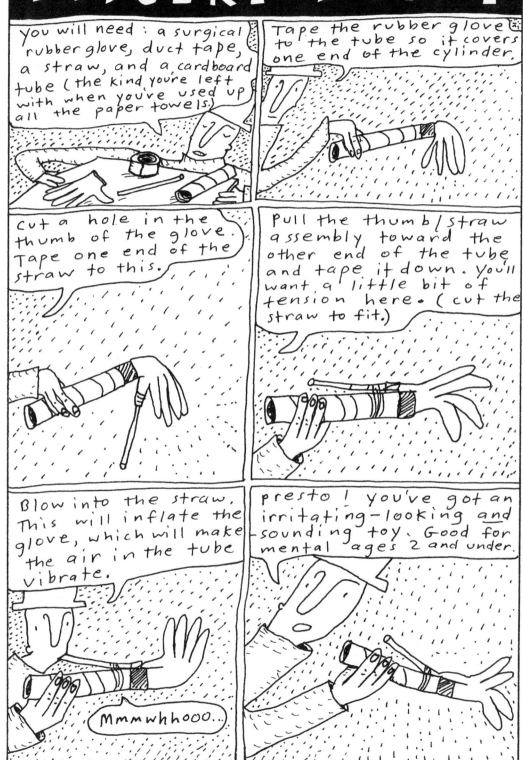

You will need: a surgical rubber glove, duct tape, a straw, and a cardboard tube (the kind you're left with when you've used up all the paper towels.)

Tape the rubber glove to the tube so it covers one end of the cylinder.

Cut a hole in the thumb of the glove. Tape one end of the straw to this.

Pull the thumb/straw assembly toward the other end of the tube and tape it down. You'll want a little bit of tension here. (cut the straw to fit.)

Blow into the straw. This will inflate the glove, which will make the air in the tube vibrate.

Mmmwhhooo...

presto! you've got an irritating-looking and sounding toy. Good for mental ages 2 and under.

STRAW SQUEAL

CHEW ON ONE END OF A STRAW UNTIL IT'S KIND OF FLAT.

BITE DOWN LIGHTLY ON THE FLAT PART WITH YOUR FRONT TEETH.

PUT GENTLE PRESSURE ON THE THROAT OF THE STRAW WITH YOUR INDEX FINGER AND THUMB. BLOW.

IF YOU GET THIS RIGHT, YOU WILL HAVE PEOPLE PLEADING WITH YOU TO STOP MAKING THE NOISE THAT COMES OUT.

WHEEE EEE!

OH MY GOD! NO!

ALTERNATING FINGER MOUTH POPPING

Taking mouth popping to an extreme, you alternate right and left index fingers in rapid-fire motion. Remember to keep lips in a tight little hoop.

Be economical with your motion. Practice with a metronome in front of your bathroom mirror.

FORCED-AIR MOUTH POPPING

A noninvasive method of mouth popping.

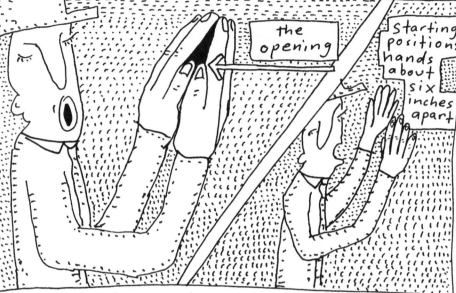

the opening

Starting position: hands about six inches apart

You smack your hands together in the manner illustrated above, but you smack them right next to your open mouth, so the opening above the thumb nails jets the compressed air of your clap into your mouth. The mouth must be held firmly, lips in a tight little hoop, as with all the mouth popping stunts.

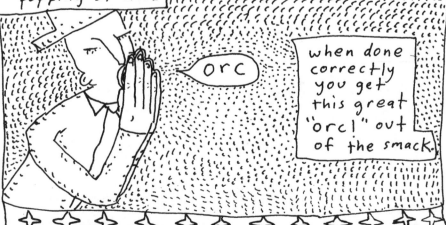

orc

when done correctly you get this great "orcl" out of the smack.

PSYCHEDELIC MOUTH

GET ABOUT A FOOT OF TRANSPARENT TAPE. PACKING TAPE WORKS GREAT.

ATTACH ONE END NEAR A CORNER OF YOUR MOUTH.

PULL THE TAPE AROUND THE BACK OF YOUR HEAD AND ATTACH THE OTHER END NEAR THE OTHER CORNER OF YOUR MOUTH.

SHOVE YOUR CHIN FORWARD AND YOUR MOUTH WILL SPREAD OPEN INTO A VERY UNNATURAL AND DISTURBING GAPE.

SHRILL STRAW

First, let me apply fair warning! I've gotten myself in trouble with this trick. The chances are you will too. O.K., go ahead.

Get yourself a glass of water and a straw. That's all you'll need

Do I need to state the obvious? This is a restaurant stunt, good in all restaurants in the lower 48.

Alright, so what you do next is suck some water into the straw and then pinch the end so the water can't escape.

SUCK **Pinch**

Now pucker up your embouchere and blow across the end of the straw while simultaneously letting the water out of the straw with your pinch hand. Let the water out slowly for best results. It should sound like a very shrill slide whistle, only louder. With the right straw you can get a sound so piercing and screachy that people will get angry at you, especially after the 69th repetition.

1. suck 2. pinch 3. blow

SCARY TEETH STUNT

CUT AN ORANGE INTO FOUR SECTIONS. EAT ONE SECTION.

TAKE THE LEFTOVER PEEL AND FLIP IT INSIDE OUT.

TAKE A KNIFE AND CUT A "MOUTH" AND "TEETH" IN THE PEEL.

WEDGE THE PEEL INTO YOUR MOUTH.

DONE CORRECTLY, YOU WILL LOOK LIKE SOMEONE WITH SCARY, HAND-CARVED TEETH.

Grasshopper Stunt

It does not hurt to put a grasshopper into your mouth.

You can go up to someone and say:

Could you make sure there are no poppy seeds stuck between my teeth?

The person will look at your teeth, as you pull your lips back, and then you'll open your mouth and the grasshopper will hop out.

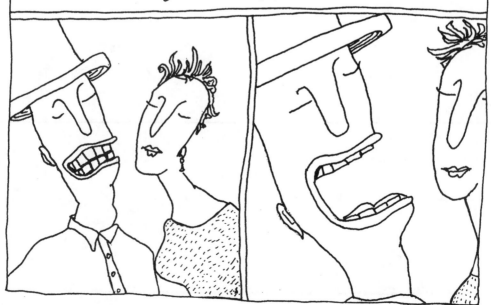

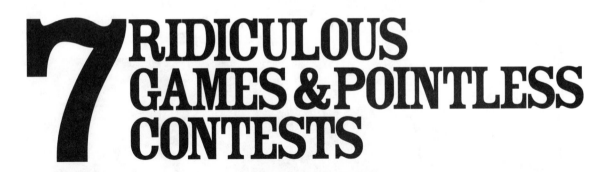

7 RIDICULOUS GAMES & POINTLESS CONTESTS

THE HUMAN TABLE

GO SIDE TO SIDE WITH A FRIEND SO SHE'S FACING ONE DIRECTION AND YOU'RE FACING THE OTHER. (YOU ARE RIGHT ARM TO RIGHT ARM.)

PUT YOUR RIGHT HAND UNDER HER LEFT ARM AND HOLD ON. (SHE DOES THE SAME.)

HOLD LEFT HANDS WITH EACH OTHER AND LIE BACKWARD ALL THE WAY. (VERY TRUSTINGLY!)

THIS STUNT CAN BE DONE RAPIDLY.

REST YOUR BACK ON THE OTHER PERSON'S RIGHT KNEE.

YOU MUST HAVE GOOD KNEES AND SOLID BACKS. BE CAREFUL!

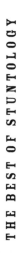

Drawing Stunt

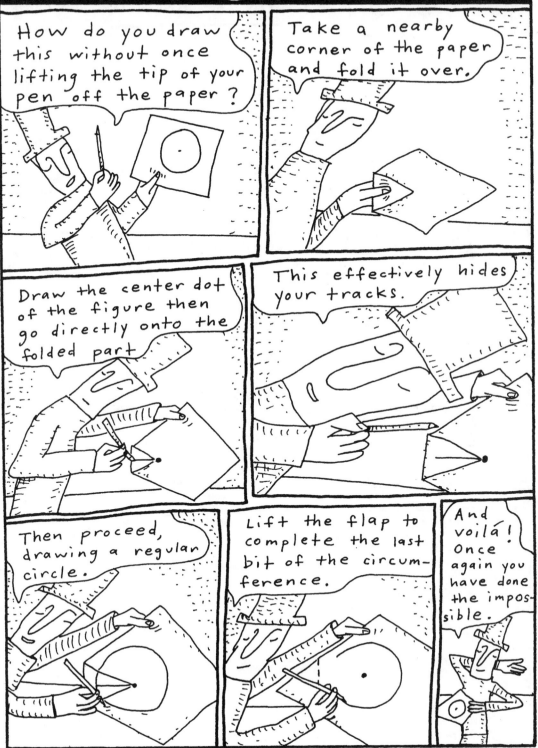

COIN-GRABBING STUNT

PUT TWO QUARTERS ON THE BACK OF YOUR HAND.

ATTEMPT TO PULL YOUR HAND OUT FROM UNDER THE COINS AND CATCH BOTH OF THEM BEFORE THEY FALL TO THE GROUND.

whoosh!

THIS IS POSSIBLE, BUT IT REQUIRES THE REFLEXES OF A BOBCAT.

AN orange had a baby

"an orange had a baby" you tell the onlookers as you take knife in hand and begin to cut its skin. "was it a boy or was it a girl?"

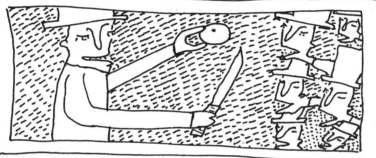

Then you cut out the outline of a human on your orange, centering the little belly button thing of the orange on the genital region.

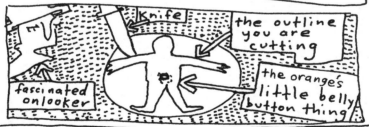

knife

the outline you are cutting

the orange's little belly button thing

fascinated onlooker

when you've finished cutting pry the outline of the human from the orange, asking onlookers "is it a boy or a girl?

Then pull the final attachment away [the little belly button thing in the genital region] and pull your human off the orange

It will either be a boy or a girl—trust me on this one folks!

DOLLAR-CATCHING STUNT

HAVE SOMEONE HOLD THEIR THUMB AND INDEX FINGER ABOUT AN INCH APART.

DANGLE A DOLLAR BILL INTO THIS GAP, SO GEORGE'S HEAD IS BETWEEN THEIR FINGERS.

SAY TO THE PERSON:

TRY TO CATCH THE BILL WHEN I LET GO OF IT.

IF YOU GET GOOD AT RELEASING THE BILL AT THE RIGHT MOMENT, IT WILL BE ALMOST IMPOSSIBLE TO CATCH IT.

Spoon Game

you'll need a small crowd of spectators and a couple of spoons.

challenge someone to a spoon hitting contest in which you have to hit your opponent on the head with a spoon held in your mouth.

Demonstrate the technique by biting on your spoon and bobbing it up and down a few times.

Let your opponent go first. He will try with comic ineffectiveness to hit you with his mouthed spoon. It is of course absolutely impossible to hit someone hard in this manner.

Then have your opponent bow his head down and you pretend to hit him on the head with your spoon. Only <u>you</u> will have a secret partner in the game, lurking behind your opponent,

and the secret partner will take <u>his</u> spoon (the third spoon you need for this stunt) and THONK your opponent on the head with it.

Ideally this will lead your opponent into thinking there is some sort of technique to the spoon game and he will subject himself to several rounds of spoonings, trying to figure out how to thonk you like you're thonking him.

THE BEST OF STUNTOLOGY

288

House Rules

At the beginning of a game of Monotony a few years ago my friend announced, "House Rules!"

House Rules!

It would be a normal game in all respects except: Everyone was to use a pseudonym,

No swearing,
Ahah ah!
poo poo stinky butt...

No pointing,

If someone left the board to get something to drink or to go to the bathroom and they failed to say, "No cheating,"

players staying could freely cheat. Anyone failing to adhere to the House Rules had to ante $100.00 into the center of the board.*

*with fake money, of course

As I recall, I lost all of my money and spent much of the game managing my friend Colin's chain of hotels.

HAND-HITTING STUNT

PUT YOUR HAND FLAT ON A TABLE. TELL SOMEONE, "GO AHEAD. HIT IT!"

THEY HIT IT. BAM!

SAY, "HIT IT HARDER. IT DOESN'T HURT." AND IT DOESN'T.

THE TABLE ABSORBS THE BLOW. IT'S AN INTERESTING STUDY IN PHYSICS. I THINK. (HAVE THEM HIT THE BODY OF YOUR HAND, NOT THE FINGERS)

"GO AHEAD. HIT IT ONE MORE TIME," YOU SAY. AND IF THEY'VE BEEN HAVING A LITTLE TOO GOOD A TIME HITTING YOUR HAND, AGAIN?

YOU SIMPLY REMOVE YOUR HAND AT THE LAST MOMENT AND LET THEIR HAND CRASH INTO THE TABLE. BAM! whhhst!

THEY'VE REALLY GOT THIS COMING TO THEM.

BOTTLE STUNT

Put a bottle upside down on top of a dollar bill.

Challenge someone to remove the dollar without touching or knocking over the bottle.

Some people will try to just flick the bill out from under the bottle, assuming it's a variation on the old tablecloth stunt.

whoosh

A fairly foolproof solution is for you to roll the bill up. Hold points A and B and roll.

A
B

This will cause the center of the rolled bill to gently push the bottle until it slides off.

The bottle must be dry for this to work.

BABY CARROT STUNT

THIS IS A STUNT THAT CAN BE EITHER A STATEMENT OR A COMPETITION.

GET A PAIR OF SUNGLASSES AND A BAG OF BABY CARROTS.

SEE HOW MANY BABY CARROTS YOU CAN SUCCESSFULLY PLACE, WEDGE, OR BALANCE ON YOUR FACE.

GO INTO A GAS STATION AND ASK DIRECTIONS.

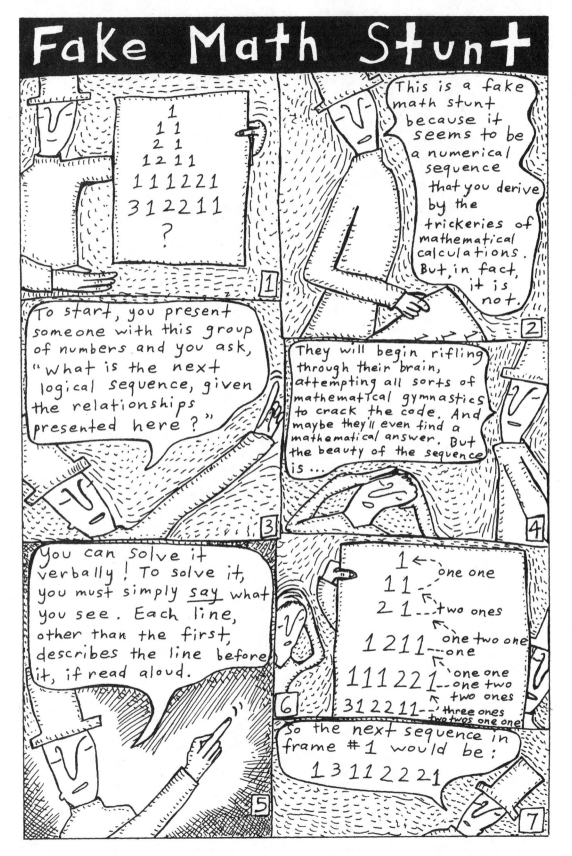

Giving The Goggles

If someone gives you "the goggles,"

you have to lie on the ground, no matter where you are, no matter what you're doing, no matter who you're with,

<u>unless</u> you are "blocking the goggles" with your hand on your cheek.

If you do not lie down immediately upon being goggled, you lose your power, and you can never play the game again.

Shopping Cart Circle Toss

If you're hanging out in a big, empty grocery store parking lot, there is an excellent game you can play.

Oh yeah, you gotta have a Frisbee, too.

One person grabs a shopping cart and gets really far away,

and the other person throws the Frisbee.

The shopping-cart-person has to try to catch the Frisbee in the cart.

The object of the game is to do this without being rammed by a car.

TAPE MEASURE STUNT

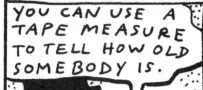

YOU CAN USE A TAPE MEASURE TO TELL HOW OLD SOMEBODY IS.

THIS IS NOT A MIND-READING FEAT, THOUGH. YOU ALSO HAVE TO KNOW WHAT YEAR THE PERSON WAS BORN.

THE TAPE MEASURE STUNT JUST SPEEDS EVERYTHING UP SO YOUR CALCULATION IS INSTANTANEOUS.

WHAT YOU DO: EXTEND THE TAPE TO THE YEAR. IF IT IS 2008, PULL THE TAPE OUT TO 108.

THEN FOLD THE TAPE IN HALF, BRINGING THE END OF THE TAPE IN LINE WITH THE 108" MARK.

THEN ASK SOMEONE WHAT YEAR THEY WERE BORN.

1927.

WITHOUT HAVING TO EMPLOY A GRAIN OF MATHEMATICAL SKILL, SIMPLY FIND 27" ON THE RULER AND THEN LOOK AT THE CORRESPONDING NUMBER ON THE OTHER SIDE OF THE TAPE. YOU SAY: "IN 2007 YOU ARE 80 YEARS OLD."

THANKS!

Thank you to all the people flung out all over the world who have taken the time to show and tell me their stunts.

SPECIFIC THANKS TO Abby Ladin, Wade Bartlett, Sue Sternberg, Danny Noveck, Rob Hayes, Nate and Ben Cooper, Dirk Powell, Chris Layer, Susan Clark, Sue London, Susan Waters, Jeremiah McLane, Ted Braun, Wild Asparagus, Peter and Elka Schumann, Bread & Puppet Theater, Peter Burns, Sherry Frazer, Atul Gawande, Jim Miller, Jennifer Bass, Jane Hamilton, Dave Barry, Ellen Bartlett, Kylie Foxx McDonald, Raquel Jaramillo, Suzie Bolotin, Robb Allen, Irene Demchyshyn, Peter Workman, Robert Meitus, Marika Partridge, David Schwartz, Ira Glass, Martha Sattinger, Sarah Stowe, Jay Ladin, Peter and Max Reit, Beth Mangum, and Martha and Richmond Bartlett.

CREDIT WHERE CREDIT IS DUE

I collect stunt ideas everywhere I go. I would like to credit the following friends, acquaintances, and correspondents for contributing material for this book.

WRITE YOUR NAME IN THE AIR WITH YOUR BUTT, page 3: P. Mangum ★ ANNOYING HEAD HUG, page 5: Nate Cooper ★ YAWNING STUNT, page 6: Suzannah Armstrong-Park ★ KNUCKLE-POCKET POPPING, page 7: Matt Gordon ★ NO-BONES STUNT, page 8: Paddy League ★ THE EXPANDING FINGER TRICK, page 10: Ruth Blackwell ★ POTATO ON THE DOOR, page 12: Liz Carroll, who wrote a tune of the same title ★ ASSISTED-WALKING STUNT, page 13: Rob Hall in 4th Grade ★ SIMULATED FLYING STUNT, page 15: Pete Sutherland and Gary Dulabaum ★ COOKIE TRICK, page 17: Georgia Rose Armstrong-Park ★ SCARY CRUNCHING STUNT, page 18: June Drucker ★ THE "DON'T-I-KNOW-YOU-FROM-SOMEWHERE?" STUNT, page 20: Jay Unger ★ COUNTING IN BINARY STUNT, page 21: Sam Amidon ★ ONE-ARMED CHANGE COUNTER, page 24: Cammy Kaynor ★ BATHROOM STUNT, page 25: Eve Podet ★ THE GRABBING HAND GAME, page 28: Nate Cooper ★ STRAW FARTING, page 31: Veronica Sampson ★ LEG HUG, page 33: Nate Cooper ★ BORING CONVERSATION TRICK, page 34: Sima Belmar ★ IRRITATING HAND-CLAPPING STUNT, page 35: Evie Ladin and Elise Witt ★ THE I.D.-10-+ MANUAL, page 37: Michael Vallient ★ CUTTING STUNT, page 46: Susan Waters ★ OPEN-A-BOTTLE-WITH-YOUR-EYE-SOCKET-STUNT, page 47: Greg Canote ★ TOOTHPICK TRICK, page 48: Hunt Mallett ★ PAPER CLIP STUNT, page 51: Rich Bartlett ★ FORK TELEKINESIS, page 52: Molly Mason ★ FAKE SWORD-SWALLOWING STUNT, page 53: Ben Cooper ★ RESURRECT A CHICKEN, page 54: Christine Balfa ★ LIGHT-A-MATCH-WITH-YOUR-FEET STUNT, page 56: Phil Gerard ★ SOMEWHAT FASCINATING CORK STUNT, page 57: Linda Handelsman ★ FIST-ON-FIST RESIST, page 59: Able Allen ★ CONTROL WATER WITH HAND ENERGY, page 60: Ariel Balter ★ "MATH" STUNT, page 61: Becky Tracy and Keith Murphy ★ FLOATING NEEDLE, page 62: Steve Elliot ★ SKEWER THROUGH A BALLOON, page 65: Jumahl ★ PICK UP A BOTTLE, page 67: Brian Perkins ★ GRINNING JACKSON STUNT, page 69: June Drucker ★ COAT HANGER TRICK, page 70: Coyote ★ PENCILS IN THE CEILING STUNT, page 71: Rick Shelburne ★ SLOW CAN CRUSH, page 72: Ben Cooper ★ NAPKIN-BALANCING STUNT, page 73: John Scott ★ PAPER STUNT, page 74: Barbara Lubell ★ QUARTER-BALANCING STUNT, page 75: Amy Bartlett ★ TABLE-LIFTING STUNT, page 76: David Howells ★ NAIL-BALANCING STUNT, page 80: Cliff Emory ★ BACK-TO-THE-WALL STUNT, page 81: Danielle Perdue ★ IMPOSSIBLE CORK STUNT, page 82: Barbara Lubell ★ CIRCUMNAVIGATING A CHAIR STUNT, page 85: Johnny Moynihan ★ SOL'S PAPER TRICK, page 86: Sol Weber ★ CAN-BALANCING STUNT, page 87: Steph Coleman ★ TRIPLE MIDDLE FINGER, page 88: Van Kaynor ★ MATCH-BLOWING STUNT, page 89: Dr. Michael Hamburger ★ DRAWING STUNT, page 90: Augustus Moebius ★ FOAM SURPRISE, page 93: John Skelton ★ PRE-SLICED BANANA, page 97: Danny Noveck ★ LARGE BLADDER STUNT, page 100: Rob Hayes ★ FUN WITH FUNNELS, page 101: Bob Childs ★ TAKE OVER A RADIO STUNT, page 103: Rick Noll ★ BELTLOOP POPPING, page 107: Christopher Layer ★ SEAT STUNT, page 108: Abby Ladin, inadvertently ★ POSTAL STUNT, page 109: Michael Meador ★ COFFEE-SPILLING STUNT, page 112: Ed Baggott ★ ADJUST-YOUR-NOSE-WITH-A-TABLE STUNT, page 114: Paco Rubenstein ★ BOXING SOMEONE IN AT A PARTY, page 116: David Ayers ★ HOTEL TRICK, page 117: Beth Butler ★ FAKE-TASTING STUNT, page 118: Mrs. Mackamer and Mr. Reed ★ BOUILLON SHOWER, page 120: Jeremiah McLane ★ GAME SHOW STUNT, page 121: Sylvie Fefer ★ BATHROOM TERRORISM, page 122: Nate Cooper ★ HAT STUNT, page 123: Amy McFarland ★ DELAYED MILK-DRIBBLE STUNT, page 124: Michael Vallient ★ HAY BALE STUNT, page 125: Rich Remsburg ★ QUARTER STUNT, page 129: Joseph Petrarca and Amy Bartlett ★ THE I-AM-TOTALLY-OBLIVIOUS STUNT, page 133: Susan Clark ★ TOLL BOOTH STUNT, page 134: Sue Sternberg ★ SQUIRTING TOILET SEAT, page 135: Steve Recchia ★ FINGER-PULLING STUNT, page 138: Abby Ladin ★ SCARE THE DRIVER, page 140: Polly Sweet ★ TRACING IMAGINARY MOOSE, page 141: Peter Burns ★ FRAMED PHOTO STUNT, page 142: Evil Diane ★ ROOM REARRANGEMENT STUNT, page 143: Banjo Boe ★ LLOYD'S FAKE FLAT TIRE, page 144: Lloyd ★ VASELINE STUNT, page 145: Amy Bartlett ★ DOCTOR'S OFFICE STUNT, page 147: Ruth Blackwell ★ SPRAYING TOILET STUNT, page 149: Jesse White ★ HUMAN RECORD PLAYER, page 152: Rich Remsberg ★

AMATEUR LEVITATION STUNT, page 156: David Howells ★ THE GAMMY LEG, page 158: Nate Cooper ★ WEIRD NEUROLOGICAL STUNT, page 159: Monica Maynard ★ WEIRD ARM SENSATION, page 163: Rosie and Suzannah Armstrong-Park ★ NASAL HEXAGON-TRACING STUNT, page 164: Jay Ladin ★ FINGER TOUCH AND SWIVEL STUNT, page 165: Julia Nickles ★ COAT HANGER BRAIN GONG, page 166: Christopher Layer ★ RING FINGER STUNT, page 167: Steve Elliot ★ ARMPIT HAIR STUNT, page 169: Kalia Kliban ★ TRIANGLE SQUARE 12-COUNT DRAWING STUNT, page 172: Lydia Spooner ★ APPLE STUNT, page 174: Nick West ★ SALAMI STUNT, page 176: Yuri Yarmolinsky ★ PANCAKE STUNT, page 178: Linda Handelsman ★ IN-THE-EAR-AND-OUT-THE-MOUTH STUNT, page 179: Paco Rubenstein ★ SIMULATED SELF-CANNIBALISM STUNT, page 182: Sean Oshima ★ FAKE BOOGER STUNT, page 183: Kalmia Traver ★ KETCHUP/COKE REVERSAL STUNT, page 184: Bob Duffy ★ BLOW-OUT-YOUR-BRAINS STUNT, page 185: Sam Allison ★ FART-RECORDING STUNT, page 186: Amelia Terry and Erin Glass ★ SNEEZING STUNT, page 188: Peter Burns ★ THE PEANUT BUTTER TOOTHPASTE TRICK, page 189: This stunt was played on the author in 1972, by John, Martha, Tom, and Uncle Bill Gold ★ CHANGE-CHANNELS-WITH-YOUR-UVULA STUNT, page 194: Mike Leonard ★ SUPERBALL BOOMERANG, page 196: Richmond Bartlett ★ STRAW WRAPPER FLAPPER, page 200: Eric Thorin ★ FRENCH FRY CATAPULT, page 201: Nate Cooper ★ CRACKER-SPINNING STUNT, page 202: Robert Orenstein ★ PUMPKIN THROW-UP STUNT, page 203: Evie Ladin ★ ROLLING PENNY STUNT, page 206: Mary Witt ★ MAGIC FINGER STUNT, page 208: Amy Bartlett ★ HAIRDO SIMULATION, page 209: Abby Ladin ★ BANANA-BREAKING STUNT, page 210: Sue Sternberg ★ SHOVING PENCILS UP YOUR NOSE, page 211: Rich Remsburg ★ SNEEZING WITH FORK, page 213: Malcolm Dalglish ★ FLYING NAPKIN STUNT, page 214: Lotte Dula ★ THE WORM, page 215: Pilar Zazu ★ ANYA'S PENCIL-SPINNING STUNT, page 216: Anya Schoenegge ★ STUNT FACE-SLAPPING, page 222: Rafe Stefanini ★ NOSE CRACKING, page 224: Martha Bartlett ★ GENETICALLY ENGINEERED BANANA STUNT, page 228: Rich Morse ★ PLANT MISSILES, page 229: Linda Handelsman ★ "R" LANGUAGE, page 234: Doug Fontein ★ NEWFOUNDLAND MUMMER'S LANGUAGE, page 236: Becky Tracy ★ BING CROSBY LANGUAGE, page 237: Sue Sternberg ★ SIMULALIA, page 238: Karen Axelrod ★ "A" LANGUAGE, page 239: Abby Ladin ★ EEFIN,' page 240: the Master Eefist, Steve Hickman ★ DO-IT-YOURSELF WATER FOUNTAIN STUNT, page 243: Danielle Perdue ★ HOW TO EAT LIKE A LIZARD, page 245: Peter Burns and Terry Bouricius ★ LEAF BOMBARDE, page 249: Chris Layer ★ AIR PASSAGEWAY STUNT, page 250: Liz and Hannah Barnum ★ GIANT BUCK TEETH, page 251: Veronica Sampson ★ THE ZURNA, page 252: Becky Ashenden and Chuck Corman ★ TRAPDOOR SQUIRTING STRAW STUNT, page 255: Mark Conkle ★ INFLATABLE MOUTH, page 256: Theodore Braun ★ TINY BOX OF RAISINS STUNT, page 257: Rob Hall ★ EXPOSED TEETH TRICK, page 258: Jimmy Leary ★ DIDGERI-DON'T, page 260: Dr. Betsy Brown ★ THE MOUTH FLUTE, page 262: John Herrmann ★ STRAW SQUEAL, page 263: Jeff Burke ★ ALTERNATING FINGER MOUTH POPPING, page 265: Robby Hall ★ FORCED-AIR MOUTH POPPING, page 266: Steve Hickman ★ PSYCHEDELIC MOUTH, page 267: Sam Allison ★ SHRILL STRAW, page 268: Susan Murphy ★ GRASSHOPPER STUNT, page 270: Phil Gerard ★ THE HUMAN TABLE, page 272: Frank Clayton ★ SPOON FOOD ROULETTE, page 273: Julia Thorton ★ HUNKER DOWN, page 274: Phil Gerard ★ LICKING CONTEST, page 275: Michael Vallient and Miki Bird ★ YES, NO, MAYBE, page 276: Peter Burns ★ SLOW BIKE RACE, page 277: Nate Cooper ★ VARIATIONS ON THE TRADITIONAL SONG "BINGO" STUNT, page 278: S. Hickman and C. Buchwald ★ DRAWING STUNT, page 279: Jeffrey Rovitz ★ STRAW WRAPPER KNOT STUNT, page 281: Adam Cavan ★ PLAYGROUND MIND GAME, page 282: Gail Larsen ★ FLIPPING GAME, page 284: Nate Cooper ★ THE PSYCHIC NINES STUNT, page 285: Karyn in Kent, Ohio ★ DUCK-BILLED PLATYSLOTH, page 287: Discovered on a Bartlett family vacation ★ SPOON GAME, page 288: Joe Herrmann ★ TIMING EXERCISE, page 291: Stan Raucher and Chris Layer ★ CEILING FAN STUNT, page 292: J. Anderson ★ HOUSE RULES, page 293: Mathias Dubelier ★ COASTER FLIPPING, page 294: Liz Barnum and Abby Ladin ★ ADVANCED COASTER FLIPPING, page 295: Liz Barnum ★ EAR-NOSE GRABBING, page 296: A. Ladin ★ CHEEK DARTS, page 298: Ellie Sharman ★ ADDING STUNT, page 300: Nate Cooper ★ TOILET-PAPER MUMMY, page 301: Wade Bartlett ★ ONION JOUSTING, page 302: Peter Burns ★ EXQUISITE CORPSE, page 303: Peter Burns ★ THE BEEPING GAME, page 304: Nate Cooper ★ BABY CARROT STUNT, page 305: mandolin genius B. Winship ★ FAKE MATH STUNT, page 307: Erika Biga ★ GIVING THE GOGGLES, page 308: Thomas Bartlett ★ SHOPPING CART CIRCLE TOSS, page 311: Ben Cooper ★ HANDKERCHIEF NOISE GAME, page 312: Claudio Buchwald ★ TAPE MEASURE STUNT, page 313: Joe Dawson via Jay Edmunds ★

13 MINI INDEXES

BIG INDEX